Free Indeed

FINDING TRUE JOY

Felicity Jayne

Copyright © 2024 by Felicity Jayne. All rights reserved.

No portion of this book may be reproduced in any form without written permission from the publisher or author except as permitted by the Copyright Act 1968.

This publication is designed to provide accurate and authoritative information in regard to the subject matter covered. While the publisher and author have used their best efforts in preparing this book, they make no representations with respect to the accuracy or completeness of the contents of this book. The advice and strategies contained herein may not be suitable for your situation. You should consult with a professional when appropriate. Neither the publisher nor the author shall be liable for any loss of profit or any other commercial damages, including but not limited to special, incidental, consequential, personal, or other damages.

Unless otherwise noted, all Scripture quotations are taken from the New International Version (NIV), NIV copyright ©1972, 1978, 1984, 2011 by Biblica, Inc. All rights reserved.

Also used: The Passions Translation, Passion & Fire Ministries, Inc, Copyright ©2020. All rights reserved.
Also used: The Message Copyright ©1993, 1994, 1995, 1996, 2000, 2001, 2002, 2018 by Eugene H Peterson. All rights reserved.
Also used: New Living Translation (NLT), Copyright © 1996, 2004, 2015 by Tyndale House Foundation. Tyndale House Publishers, Inc., Carol Stream, Illinois 60188. All rights reserved.
Also used: New King James Version (NJKV), Copyright © 1982 by Thomas Nelson. All rights reserved.
Also used: English Standard Version (ESV), ESV Text Edition: 2016. Copyright © 2001 by Crossway Bibles, a publishing ministry of Good News Publishers.
Also used: Christian Standard Bible, (CSB), Copyright © 2017 by Holman Bible Publishers. All rights reserved.

If you would like to purchase any further copies of this book, please contact Ingram Spark Australia or www.felicityjayne.com.

For further copies of Free Indeed place an order at felicityjayne.com

Trade paper back ISBN 978-1-7637951-4-3
ePUB ISBN: 978-1-7637951-0-5
1st edition, 2024, printed in Australia.

John 8 v 36

So if the Son sets you free,

you will be **Free indeed**

To my loving husband, who is the
most inspiring and supportive person in my life,
my beautiful and precious children,
my glorious grandson,

and

for every reader who finds themselves
in the pages of this book.

Contents

1. Finding Rest — 1
2. God's Beloved Child — 13
3. My Heavenly Father — 23
4. Truly Loved — 31
5. Well of Life — 49
6. Asking God — 61
7. Be Bold — 69
8. Loving Others — 75
9. The Embrace — 91
10. Dream Life — 107
11. Are You Worried — 127
12. Be Still — 135
13. Singing in the Wilderness — 145
14. Living in Paradise — 159

15. Finding Peace 171
16. Set Free 185

CHAPTER ONE

Finding Rest

I want to share with you some of the most powerful experiences of my life. Amid trauma and pain, I was able to find true rest - rest for my soul.

If you are anything like me, you love to get comfortable when reading. My little house is on the side of a cliff overlooking the ocean. I have a beautiful, faded, worn velvet armchair in my upstairs room, which I love curling up in when reading. My choice is always the Word of God, different books on theology, women's ministry, faith, hope and healing. I sit next to a window where the sun shines in, and I love to feel the warmth of its rays on my face.

As I read, I have a beautiful blanket over my lap, a cuppa and a cold drink, so I can settle in for hours. So, before you begin this story of redemption, healing and finally freedom, I ask you to make sure you are comfortable too. For my sake, find a soft or warm blanket, a hot or cold beverage, or maybe both, just like me.

I will begin my story now that you are settled, but I do want to prepare you. Sometimes, these words may be hard to read, but it is important, so please be patient with me. I promise this book has an incredible testimony of God's goodness and lessons to learn for everyone.

Most mornings, I begin my day by going for a glorious walk along the beach, and this morning was like many others. I would quietly pray or sing as the ocean spray and wind would blow all around me. It's always been my secret place with God. I would pray for my family and ask God's revelation for the ladies attending my monthly Bible study. Due to my home's location; I would walk down a steep path, around an isolated hill, and then onto a rocky beach. I would then cross a boat ramp, which would lead to a beautiful sandy strip of beach where I could stride for up to an hour one way.

This morning as I crossed the boat ramp, I noticed it was completely empty; I realised a storm must be coming. It was very unusual; generally, by 7 am, quite a few well-worn fishermen were on the water, and their cars and trailers were already in the carpark. This day, there was none. As I reached the entrance to the beach, I looked into the dunes and saw a figure crouching in the sand. I felt an overwhelming sense of dread, which was strange, as I always loved greeting people and their accompanying dogs as they enjoyed my local beach.

At that moment, the figure stood up and started charging towards me. There was a low wire fence between us, which they jumped quickly over and came running chaotically and aggressively my way. They were yelling and calling me the very worst names you can call a woman, which will not be repeated in this book. As this person came closer, I realised she was a woman. She seemed angry, disoriented, and struggling with reality.

As I tried to de-escalate the situation, she yelled that she was going to kill me over and over again. I looked around for someone to help, but still, the beach was deserted, and the carpark was empty. Again, I tried to reason with her, but she continued pacing and ranting. With a flash of her fist, she punched me in the face. I staggered and fell backwards, but thankfully, not enough to fall entirely to the ground. I tried to escape her, but I couldn't. She was all around me; somehow I instinctively knew I mustn't turn my back on her. If I started to run, she could effortlessly chase me down, and the only path back to my home was a deserted and isolated one. She continued to encircle and lunge towards me like a boxer trying to intimidate their opponent. I was in real danger.

To give you context, I was in my late forties and expecting my first grandchild. I was of average build (some would say more generous), with no fighting or martial arts skills whatsoever. I later learnt this woman was a personal trainer in her early thirties and, unfortunately, high on methamphetamines. She had a clinical diagnosis of schizophrenia and was in the middle of a psychotic episode.

I remember trying to adjust my fist, thinking I may need

to defend myself, but feeling **incredibly weak**. Was it thumbs in or out to punch someone? Who was I kidding? I had never punched anyone in my life! From the small amount of time in this woman's presence, I perceived this was possibly not her first fight.

This is when the Holy Spirit repeated Paul's words:

"For, when I am weak, then I am strong."

2 Corinthians 12 v 10 NIV

Immediately, as I began to lift my hands and adjust my fists, I instead opened my palms, and began to pray. I knew it was high stakes and switched to praying in the Holy Spirit language. We continued in this state for what seemed like a long time. In this awkward dance, she continued to circle behind me for a better vantage point. I just continued to raise my hands, pivoting and praying and refusing her access to my back and neck. When you think of it, it is a great model for life - pivoting and praying.

Anyway, to continue the story, this caused her no end of frustration. Finally, she recoiled back, once, twice and then a third time, as she tried to hit me. Miraculously, her fist didn't make contact with my face or body.

Now, I apologise to anyone who struggles with the supernatural. I will relay this story truthfully, just as it happened. The third time, she recoiled, her head tilted to the side most unusually. Her blue eyes turned black as the night, and she said in the loudest, deepest growl, "Stop what you are doing!" With that, she pulled out a short, sharpened metal stake and thrust it at my side.

Now, I knew I was going to die. It is the strangest feeling to face your mortality in such a violent way. I want to say that I thought, "God, take me; I am ready", but that was not what I was feeling at all. The thought of my family suffering and finding my body in such a horrific manner was utterly terrifying.

My life flashed before me. I thought, "Oh no, why God, is this how I die?" I had always imagined dying in my early nineties in a charming little nursing home, with worship music playing and generations of my children singing as I entered God's gates. Instead, I am going to die violently, stabbed to death on an isolated part of the beach! I could not believe this was going to be my story. It was only two weeks until my beautiful daughter was due to give birth to my baby grandson, and I remember saying to God, "I can't die today; my family needs me!" Let's be honest; I am sure most women would feel the same; we are all juggling so much in life, with so many people needing our help or care.

Now, just to put your mind at ease, and as you can probably guess, I didn't die. I have never had quick reflexes or any sporty abilities whatsoever, so as she lunged forward with her weapon in hand, I closed my eyes tight and yelled, "Help me, God!" I don't know if God moved me or moved her arm, but her aim shifted and grazed just past my hip. I called out to God – "God, help me!" Again, I longingly looked at the vacant carpark, praying someone would come. Then, a miracle happened; suddenly, one solitary car pulled into the car park. I couldn't believe it. She went to lunge the weapon into my side again, I realised I needed to run!

Now, in my recollection, I ran faster than any middle-aged woman has ever run before, wearing thongs on sand. A few weeks later, while speaking with the police, and to my disappointment, I noticed on the security footage that it might have been slightly slower. I was so terrorised that when I reached the stranger's car, I opened the passenger door and hopped straight in. I began slapping at the bottom of the window to lock it. I was trying to find any way to protect myself from her opening the door. To the surprise of this stranger sitting in the driver's seat, I yelled loudly, "Start the car, drive! She is trying to kill me, and she will kill us both!" This shocked, panicked, older man looked at me, and then looked at her running towards us, and thankfully sped away. He called triple 000, and within a noticeably short space of time, the police arrived. To understand the magnitude of this situation, when this woman was finally arrested, she had such strength and determination it took six police officers to arrest and place her on the ground.

I remember feeling so grateful to God and especially the Holy Spirit as He advocated in prayer and miraculously protected me from harm. I was safe and alive.

Now, I know this is not an everyday experience, but as I tell it, there is still more to this incredible story. The following Saturday, my husband and I took Kim, my God-sent getaway driver, out for lunch to thank him for saving my life. As we shared a meal, I told him I was a woman of faith. I believed God put him in that car park that day to save my life. He looked at me wide-eyed; he paused as a tear rolled down his cheek and said, "You know what, Felicity? I actually believe you. I never wake up early, and I mean never! I have lived by the beach for the past ten years and have never desired to walk along it. But that day, I woke up early, before 7 am, having an overwhelming desire to head to the ocean."

I smiled, and he then began to tell me a heartfelt story of his own. Many years earlier, when he was a younger man, he and his Dad would go to the local pub. This was something they did most nights. They would both work a long day, and would stop to have a drink. Kim (my God-sent getaway driver) made the decision to head home early. He leaned over and yelled, "Time to go, Dad", but his Father wanted to stay a little longer and chose to go home with a friend. Sadly his Dad and friend were involved in a car accident and tragically passed away that night.

For over 50 years, this beautiful man had lived with the guilt of leaving his Dad that fateful night. He mentioned his hefty regret, feeling responsible for this tragic situation. He then leant into me and said ever so quietly, "But that day when I saw you at the beach, and I helped you get away from that woman, I remember feeling this overwhelming sense of peace and rest. I truly believe that my Dad was looking down at me, saying, I am proud of you, son." I looked at Kim and hugged him; I saw God performing a miraculous work in him.

Now, I know you might be thinking this is where this story

might end, but it doesn't. I did get to write a victim impact statement to advocate to the Judge for the woman in court. I asked for her to receive rehabilitation and mercy rather than a prison sentence. I spoke of my faith, love, and support for women like her.

What was interesting was something else began to happen shortly after this traumatic event. I suddenly felt incredibly unsafe. Even though I was so grateful for God's protection, my mind struggled to process such a traumatising memory. When this event happened, I did nothing to contribute to the violence that came my way. I found it hard to trust people. I worried that some other member of the community might want to hurt me. I remember having panic attacks in the local shops. I would suffer from night and day terrors and constant flashbacks – I subconsciously found myself wanting to stay home because it was safe, away from others. I was living in a nightmare.

I sat in my beautiful, worn velvet armchair, praying to God. How could I ever feel safe, and how could I protect myself?

I questioned whether I would ever be me again, fearless, fun, and free.

I realised I had two choices:

1. I could continue to sit at home in my pyjamas with the front roller shutters down for security (in the middle of the day), watching an obscene amount of Netflix to distract my mind and eating Cadbury chocolate,

or

2. I could start reminding myself of who I am.

"I am a beloved daughter of the living God. I have not been given the spirit of fear but of power, love and a sound mind".

Immediately, I had a physical reaction to this scripture, like stepping into a warm, comforting bath filled with honey. I felt peace for the first time since the incident. I searched for other scriptures relating to overcoming fear. I found another in:

Isaiah 43 v 1–3 ESV

**"Fear not, for I have redeemed you;
I have called you by name; you are mine.**

When you pass through the waters,
I will be with you;
and through the rivers,
they shall not overwhelm you;
when you walk through the fire,
you shall not be burned,
and the flame shall not consume you."

This scripture reminded me that my God stooped down and called me by name – He was protecting me. I had nothing to fear. As I began to renew my mind, I would replace and exchange the negative identity and traumatic messages with God's truth. I remember these verses becoming my lifeblood, and I would quietly quote them as I began to feel a panic attack coming on.

One pivotal moment came in church when I was worshipping. Unfortunately, I had also lost my sense of safety and security there. Instead of praying and leaning into God's presence, I left one eye open, checking my surroundings and all the people around me – so I could be prepared for anything that might come my way.

All of a sudden, the Holy Spirit gave me a thought:

1 John 4 v 18 NKJV

"There is no fear in love, but **perfect love casts out all fear.**"

That is right - perfect love casts out all fear. I immediately experienced another flashback of that fateful day. I could see her dark eyes and her face lunging towards me, but this time, it was different. I unconsciously captured the thought. I paused, and then something miraculous happened: Jesus appeared. It was amazing. The vulnerable and traumatised woman was there, but this time, Jesus stood between us. Instead of attacking me, she ran into Jesus' arms. I saw her break down and cry. I watched her share the story of her life, the pain, the struggle and the trauma. She wept as Jesus held her.

As I watched this happen, the struggle to feel safe and panic left me, and security flooded back into my body. I felt true empathy for her and found a well of forgiveness that began to heal my heart. I felt free — free from fear and terror.

I want to acknowledge that there will be people reading this chapter who may be facing fear, trauma, or the battle of their lives. I want to encourage you – don't give up. I promise you will find hope and healing in these pages. For those of you who are new to faith or unfamiliar with God, I want to encourage you too. These pages have words of wisdom for everyone.

So, I ask you to come with me on a journey to fall in love with Jesus for the first time or all over again. I pray you will find peace, joy, and healing. I pray that my shared wisdom and stories will profoundly encourage you. I pray you will discover the **REST** the Bible speaks of, and your heart so desperately desires.

It reminds me of the scripture used as the basis of this book

Who the Son sets free is

Free Indeed

CHAPTER TWO

God's Beloved Child

Understanding who we are, and who God is, is one of the most essential parts of our life, especially a Christian one. Wrong thinking in this area can cause great heartache. We can believe, if we suffer trauma or pain, that God is somehow punishing us or that He doesn't care. I often meet people who are "stuck" in their life. Sometimes, this can be because they unconsciously create their own version of God. They can consider God more like a fictional Father Christmas, as they place their wishes before Him and expect God to answer every prayer. You will find this kind of person or this kind of Christian continually questioning God and their faith because they believe God and the world revolves around their desires and wants. They believe that they should have a truly blessed life, which is true, but on their terms, not God's.

If they do struggle or fail, it is somehow their fault; they are not praying hard enough or, even worse, maybe God is ignoring or punishing them. What a terrible way to live and what a terrible God to serve. They are continually disappointed when He doesn't deliver to their expectations and are filled with shame or guilt for not meeting His high standards or performance-based love.

Another distortion of God's character is the Vending Machine God — the idea that if you provide just the right amount of prayer, tithes, and serving, you should be able to somehow "manipulate" God to answer your wants and needs. This again adds a heaviness to serving and worshipping God, often leading to burnout. You will usually find these people as rule followers, falsely believing that following these rules will protect them from harm. They unconsciously try to find a recipe to live in an uncontrollable world where they can feel safe and secure. Their trust is not in God but in the rules that they follow. The wisdom I always turn to is found in:

Proverbs 3 v 5 NKJV

> "Trust in the Lord with all your heart
> lean not to your own understanding,
> in all your ways, acknowledge him,
> and He shall direct your paths."

Many of us love this scripture but would rather it say:

> "Trust in the Lord with all my heart,

as I lean on my **OWN** understanding,
I will acknowledge him
but also want recognition for everything I do,
and
**I will direct my own paths.
THANKS!"**

When we hold this belief, life can be difficult and stressful. The truth is that any relationship without trust cannot flourish. Its very existence will leave you feeling insecure, unsafe, and anxious. This, in turn, makes it hard to feel emotionally connected to God.

As a demonstration of this, I have two examples of people who believe in God.

The first believes in **God but does not trust Him.** She or he hopes to go to Heaven but will struggle to find joy, peace and rest. Their life will be difficult; they may feel unfulfilled and rejected and struggle to connect to God.

The second person **loves God and trusts God.** They will trust His grace and know they are going to Heaven, but will also experience Heaven here on earth, an abundant life, a life of rest, a life of gratitude, a life of connection to God and others. There will be times when they will also struggle, just like the first person, but they will continue to renew their mind and faith to remember the power and glory of God. They don't try to control others; they trust God and His wisdom, and when they find themselves in times of trouble, they trust in God and His goodness to help them through. Another scripture is found in:

John 10 v 10 NKJV

"The thief does not come except to steal, and to kill, and to destroy. **I have come that they may have life, and that they may have it more abundantly.**"

This abundant life means gaining a Heavenly perspective of life itself and growing in trust and knowledge of God. It means blossoming into a life full of the fruits of the spirit—love, joy, peace, patience, kindness, goodness, faithfulness, gentleness, and self-control — a truly wonderful way to live.

We mustn't mistake a natural expectation of success or abundance with the scripture's version of the abundant life. We are discussing the contrast between having a new car or large house, popularity, or financial security and the deep, profound needs only our spirit desires: finding rest, knowing your worth, using your talents to love others, and finding a deep-seated love that never leaves you.

To explain this further, I sometimes suggest our theological and emotional image of God can be at odds. You may say that you believe in a God of love and grace (theological understanding), but your emotional image of God is He has exceptionally high standards and is hard to please. Your head says one thing, but your heart says another. You may run to God with your mind but run away from Him with your heart.

It is interesting to note that your private emotional image

of God can often relate to your own self-image. We sometimes create the type of God we think we deserve, not the true biblical version we receive in His Word.

Remember, God is not who we think He is. He is who He says He is!

Interestingly, we form an emotional understanding of our own identity and self as children. As we grow, we receive identity messages from authority figures in the most informative years of our lives. These messages can be from our parents, our teachers, older friends, and family. They can be both negative and positive. As we move through life, some of these negative identity messages stick and can become unhelpful. When we hear these same messages spoken over us as adults, we can be triggered and go into an emotional spin. We turn to coping strategies to deal with feelings of inadequacy, rejection, guilt or shame. These could be many and varied and can range from harmful addictions, to toxic relationships, food (overeating or under-eating), seeking knowledge, excessive exercise, and unhelpful serving or working schedules. Anything to feel better about ourselves, blocking out the painful thoughts and negative emotional patterns.

Not all the previous coping strategies mentioned are bad, but they will only temporarily satisfy our deep and profound desire to find love, acceptance, and forgiveness. None of these coping strategies will deal with the root cause of the problem: our beliefs about ourselves and God.

For example, some people may feel that - I am not good

enough because they were made to feel so when they were young. Another common negative identity message might be - I am a failure or unloved. If you have received some of these messages, I am genuinely sorry.

As I talk to people, I often uncover some of these negative identity messages and work to loosen their power, exchanging and renewing their minds for God's truth.

So, moving forward, it is important that instead of letting our thoughts go into an emotional spin, reaching unconsciously for a coping mechanism or an idol, we begin to actively take control of our mind, reminding ourselves of God's truth and our true identity in Christ. Some biblical examples of this are:

Romans 12 v 2 NIV

"Do not conform to the pattern of this world,
but be transformed by renewing your mind.
Then, you will be able to test and approve
what God's will is,
his good, pleasing, and perfect will."

2 Corinthians 10 v 5 NIV

Paul says we should:
"Take captive every thought
to make it obedient to Christ."

Galatians 2 v 20 NIV

"I have been crucified with Christ;
and I no longer live, but Christ lives in me."

2 Corinthians 5 v 17 NKJV

"Therefore, if anyone is in Christ,
he is a new creation;
old things have passed away;
behold, all things have become new."

Do we believe Christ is capable of incredible things? Therefore, if Christ lives in you, and you are a new creation, you are capable of much more than you can possibly imagine.

The position is not whether Christ lives in you. He does. It is whether you believe it!

As we move through the next couple of chapters, I will teach you how to exchange the enemy's lies for God's truth, remind you of who you are and who God is and how to lean into your identity in Christ.

If you are struggling on a journey of trauma, reach out; do not hide away. Do not let this define you. You are so much more than the trauma you have suffered. Remember, be kind to yourself with lots of self-care and **renew your**

mind with God's truth. It will help to set you free and remind you to re-discover your true, authentic self, the most powerful version of you, through your identity found in God.

Having patience, as well as plenty of self-compassion, can make an enormous difference. Recovering from trauma takes time, as everyone heals at their own pace, but if months have passed and your symptoms are not letting up, be brave; you may need professional help from a trauma expert or Christian counsellor. **I will be praying for you.**

CHAPTER THREE

My Heavenly Father

Now, I want to take you back to the 1970s. My parents were young and married; I was just a tiny baby. My beautiful Mum was in her twenties, and my Dad was working on the beat as a police officer. They had been married for over a year and had purchased and renovated their first home.

By God's destiny, this house was opposite a local church pastor. Every time my parents would go out onto their front lawn, they would be greeted by a friendly older man watering his garden. He would strike up a conversation which would inevitably turn to God. During one of these conversations, my Father agreed to attend a church meeting.

After my parents attended these gatherings for six weeks,

they promised each other they would not return (no matter how much this lovely man would encourage them). While Dad was relaxing at what he thought was the last church meeting he would ever attend, the Holy Spirit moved on Mum.

When the message finished, they called for a prayer line. My Mother stood up and headed to the front of the church for prayer. She heard about Jesus' baptism and wanted to follow His example. That moment was powerful, and immediately, she was filled with the Holy Spirit. This was to the shock and horror of my Father, who was contemplating what he could *now* accomplish on a Sunday afternoon. After much consideration and seeing and hearing Mum filled with the Holy Spirit, he, too, was baptised.

This moment changed everything for our family and became a pivotal part of our faith and life. My beautiful Mum had an incredible and powerful encounter with God. If you ever have the opportunity to meet her, you will notice she is pretty shy and does not like to be the centre of attention. Still, the calling of God was so strong in her life that she found all the courage she required and could only respond to God's invitation.

Nearly two years later, my Mum was in the first trimester of her second pregnancy when she contracted Rubella - German measles. Rubella is a contagious viral infection best known for its distinctive red rash. This infection causes mild or no symptoms in most people. However, it can cause severe problems for unborn babies during early pregnancy. Mum had become aware of this virus and its consequences earlier in her life, as she knew a family whose daughter was born with significant physical complications due to its impact.

In the 1970s, my mother's family doctor explained the risks to the baby and encouraged her to terminate the pregnancy. Much to her GP's concern, my mother refused. She was immediately filled with peace and a surety God would intervene and keep her baby healthy. She went home and prayed to God, trusting in His goodness and faithfulness, and was filled with confidence and peace for the remainder of the pregnancy.

When my sister was born, she was perfect and completely healthy. The family GP who attended the birth remarked to Mum he had not expected this and agreed it was a miracle. My sister now happens to be one of the most beautiful girls I know, with an incredible love for serving God, so all praise and glory goes to God.

Just a few months earlier, there was an outbreak of Murray Valley Encephalitis (MVE) in Australia, resulting in severe illness and numerous deaths. The symptoms include fever, drowsiness, confusion, headaches, neck stiffness, nausea, tremors, and seizures. In some people, symptoms worsen due to meningitis - inflammation of the brain and spinal cord lining. My Father unfortunately found himself in hospital gravely ill, with suspected meningitis. That night, as his symptoms raged, Dad packed in ice with a fan blowing on him to reduce his high temperature, he prayed to God. He had no medication and was awaiting a definite diagnosis. He asked for deliverance and total healing of his body. He testifies of the exact moment when he knew he was totally and miraculously healed. It was only later, after prior blood tests were taken, it was revealed that he had indeed suffered from Murray Valley Encephalitis.

These two testimonies were shared with me as a young child, and they gave me confidence and understanding that God was real and present in my life and family. He was powerful and able to heal. Our parents were very young Christians when these miracles occurred, and these experiences helped to establish their faith.

Now I want to share a story of my own. When I was in my early twenties, I had two little children. My oldest came down with a fever, but after two days and two nights of giving Panadol regularly, she remained very unwell. I decided to take her to our local hospital. As we arrived, I had great faith in the doctors and nurses to help her. I spent two nights on the rollaway bed, breastfeeding my baby and looking after my sick daughter. My Husband would come in the day to help.

After the second day, with her temperature still dangerously high, and medicating with a range of antibiotics, the doctors approached the bed. They were very concerned about her persistent high temperature and had no answers on how to treat her. They discussed possible organ damage if she continued to remain in this febrile state.

After their discussion, I felt like the whole world was falling from underneath me. I needed to breathe, so I excused myself to another room and found a quiet place to pray.

As I began, I couldn't express the pain of my sorrow. I would have given everything and anything to see her healed. All I could manage was to quietly pray in the Holy Spirit language. My heart was broken. As I knelt in that room, I asked my God for comfort and randomly opened my old Bible. I placed my hand on the page and began to read, and right there in front of me was this scripture.

Mark 1 v 30 – 31 NIV

"Now Simon's mother-in-law was in bed
with a fever,
and they immediately told Jesus about her.
So, he went to her, took her hand and
helped her up.
The fever left her,
and she began to wait on them."

Please understand that I did not know this scripture. I didn't realise that the word fever was even used in the Bible. I closed it and opened it again, thinking maybe I was dreaming. I was exhausted, but in black and white was the living and breathing Word in all its glory.

I could not believe it and re-read it; at that moment, when my heart cried out to God, He spoke to me in a powerful and personal way. It was like He was sitting right alongside me, saying,

> "My precious girl,
> I am here with you; I hear you."

It was only moments later that my phone rang; it was my husband, who was sitting with my daughter next to her hospital bed. "She is healed!" he said.

Even though I was in a different location than my daughter and husband, God heard my cry. My daughter had laid in bed for four days, struggling to sit, eat or speak. She was now running around the paediatric hospital ward, skipping and singing. She didn't know I was praying for her –

But Jesus did.

CHAPTER FOUR

Truly Loved

How often do we find ourselves empty, broken, anxious or worried? Life and people let us down. God has designed us all with deep and profound spiritual needs. These needs can only truly be fulfilled by God, but how often do we find ourselves looking somewhere else or to someone else to fulfil them? We would all recognise and know the need for:

Love
Acceptance
Significance
Security
Assurance

But when we seek these spiritual needs through God, we receive one final spiritual need fulfilled:
Rest

Do we ever see ourselves or others looking for these precious spiritual needs through relationships with other broken people or through accumulating resources, both of which have the promise to fade away?

It is interesting because as we trust people to fill our deep spiritual desires, we place unrelenting pressure on the relationship or the person to be our all. They unwittingly become the centre of our lives and, in some way, a god-like feature in our existence. In the back of our minds, there is always the unconscious nagging anxiety that they could leave us by choice or tragedy, which fills our hearts with concern and anxiety. They become our everything. No one person on this planet could ever provide for our level of need, which only God can fill.

Maybe we have already given up on people and just prefer to buy the next shiny thing to find acceptance, security, or significance, to look the part to others. We might find validation in their admiration, but deep down, we still feel empty. We long for connection, our soul doesn't find rest; our thoughts ruminate, and we are filled in those quiet moments with thoughts of loneliness, regret, and possibly even despair.

We build the foundation of our lives on something that is not certain or guaranteed, so we begin to feel anxious and worried. If that is you today, I want to encourage you. You may find it hard to seek and connect to a God you do not know. There is good news because the Bible reveals God's true nature to us. We can begin to understand who He is and what His intention is for our lives. While studying, I came across this important demonstration of God's character. Let me show you:

In 1 John 4 v 8, we read -

"God is Love"

When I talk to people who may be stuck in their faith or doubt God's character, I like to refer them to this passage. It reminds each of us we are safe with God. We can sit in His presence knowing we are truly loved, truly chosen, truly forgiven, and truly accepted. When I face times of loss, sorrow or pain, I have appreciated considering this promise of God,

Psalms 34 v 18 NIV

"The Lord is closest to the brokenhearted.
He rescues those whose spirits are crushed."

I continue to renew my mind, even when I find myself suffering through sickness, pain and sorrow in this imperfect world with imperfect people, that my God loves me. When I consider the word "Love", I turn to the Bible to find its definition - the perfect verse for this is:

1 Corinthians 13 v 4-7 NIV

"Love is patient, love is kind.
It does not envy, it does not boast,
it is not proud.

It does not dishonour others,
it is not self-seeking,

it is not easily angered,
and it keeps no record of wrongs.

Love does not delight in evil
but rejoices in truth.

It always protects,
always trusts, always hopes,
always perseveres."

If we consider that "**God is Love**", as in 1 John 4 v 8, then we can emotionally exchange the word "Love" for "God" and discover the true nature of our God. We can read this text with new joy as it begins to uncover the true heart of the Father. Let's read it again:

God is **patient**; God is **kind**.
He does not envy, He does not boast;
He is not proud. He does not dishonour others,
He is not self-seeking, **God is not easily angered**,
God keeps no record of wrongs.
God does not delight in evil but rejoices in truth.
He always protects, always trusts, always hopes, always perseveres.

In the Passions translation, we read:

"Love is large and incredibly patient.
Love is gentle and consistently kind to all.

It refuses to be jealous
when a blessing comes to someone else.

Love does not brag about one's achievements
nor inflate its own importance.

Love does not traffic in shame and disrespect
nor selfishly seek its own honour.

Love is not easily irritated or quick to take offence.

Love joyfully celebrates honesty
and finds no delight in what is wrong.

Love is a safe place of shelter,
for it never stops believing the best for others."

When we truly understand God's character, we are set free from trying to please or be controlled by others. We understand God's nature and trust His goodness.

This demonstration brings great revelation. It reminds us that we can believe in an amazing and powerful God who stoops down to love us personally. Take a moment, pause, and reflect on this beautiful scripture.

Romans 8 v 14-17 TPT

> "The mature children of God
> are those who are moved
> by the impulses of the Holy Spirit.
>
> And you did not receive the
> 'spirit of religious duty,' leading you back into the
> **fear of never being good enough.**
>
> But you have received the
> 'Spirit of full acceptance,'
> enfolding you into the family of God.
>
> And you will never feel orphaned,
> for as he rises up within us,
> our spirits join him
> in saying the words of tender affection,
> 'Beloved Father!'
>
> For the Holy Spirit makes God's fatherhood,
> real to us as he
>
> **whispers into our innermost being,
> You are God's BELOVED child!"**

This verse from the passion's translation whispers into our hearts, into our deepest spiritual needs to feel loved and accepted.

One of the most important messages we can receive from God is to know who we are in Him. Examining our identity as "His BELOVED child" is one of my favourite topics to discuss.

So often, we allow other broken people to define our worth and value, and we begin to repeat these messages over and over until we believe them as truth. Many times, I meet people who have given others the power to impact their sense of belief in themselves, their value, and their worth.

As you read this book, I hope to replace or exchange these negative identity messages with God's truth. I ask, when we sit in crisis, are you sitting in a place of despair or from a place of prayer?

We still have one important choice when we believe all other choices have been taken away. Do we sit in a pit, a pit of depression, or do we sit in the power, the power of God? Do we actively exchange the lies we tell ourselves with God's goodness and truth?

These are just a few of the wrong or harmful identity messages we may speak over our lives:

I am a failure
I am not good enough
My needs do not matter
I am not worthy
I am unlovable

It is essential to recognise that these lies can control our actions and emotions. They can keep us small and stop us from stepping into everything God wants our lives to be.

The next time you hear yourself speaking like this, I challenge you to capture the thought and replace it with God's truth. The Bible is like a love letter from home. We must cherish its words because it reminds us of our authentic selves, the most powerful version of who we are. Here are some examples of the lies we may tell ourselves; you may recognise a few:

I am a failure

The spiritual need we seek is Acceptance. When we speak these words, we must stop and capture the thought. We must be curious and ask who or what do I seek my spiritual need of Acceptance in. It will most undoubtedly be from another broken person. God would never speak like this to you. Remind yourself this is not God's truth. Let's hear what God says about you:

Psalms 37 v 23-25 NLT

> "The Lord directs the steps of the godly
> He delights in every detail of their lives.
> Though they stumble,
> they will not fall,
> for the Lord holds them by the hand."

I am not good enough

The spiritual need we seek is Significance and Acceptance. Let's capture this thought again and replace it with God's truth.

Romans 8 v 14-15 TPT

"The mature children of God
are those who are moved by
the impulses of the Holy Spirit.

And you did not receive the
"spirit of religious duty,"
leading you back into the fear of
never being good enough.

But you have received the
"Spirit of full acceptance,"
enfolding you into the family of God."

My needs don't matter

The spiritual need we seek in others is Assurance.

Psalms 147 v 3 NIV

"God heals the broken-hearted
and binds their wounds."

Psalms 34 v 18 NIV

"The Lord is close to the broken-hearted
and saves those who are crushed in spirit."

John 3 v 17 NIV

"For God did not send
His Son into the world to condemn the world,
but to save the world through Him."

I am not worthy

The spiritual need we seek is Acceptance.

Ephesians 3 v 20 TPT

"Never doubt God's almighty power
to work in you and accomplish all this.
He will achieve infinitely more
than your greatest request,
your most unbelievable dream
and exceed your wildest imagination!
He will outdo all,
for his miraculous power
constantly energises you."

I am unlovable

The spiritual need we seek here is obviously Love. But what does God say about His love for you?

Romans 8 v 38 TPT

"So now I live with the confidence
that there is nothing in the universe
with the power to separate us from God's love."

Ephesians 3 v 16-19 TPT

"And I pray that he would unveil
within you the unlimited riches of his glory
and favour until
supernatural strength floods
your innermost being
with His divine might and explosive power.

Then, by constantly using your faith,
the life of Christ will release inside you,
and the resting place of His love
will become the very
source and root of your life."

"Then you will be empowered to discover
what every holy one experiences,

**the great magnitude of the astonishing
love of Christ in all its dimensions.**

How deeply intimate
and far-reaching is His love!

How enduring and inclusive it is!

Endless love beyond measure that
transcends our understanding,
this extravagant love pours into you
until you are filled to overflowing,
with the fullness of God."

How beautiful. These are just a few pearls of wisdom that God wants to hide in our hearts. I have these scriptures all around my home to remind me of His promises and my identity in Him. What are some other thoughts we may need to address?

I need to be in control

The spiritual need we seek is Rest for our mind, body and soul. This true rest is only ever found in the Heavenly Father, as I mentioned before:

Matt 11 v 28 MSG

"Are you tired? Worn out?
Burned out on religion?

Come to me. Get away with me,
and you will recover your life.

I will show you how to take a real rest.
Walk with me and work with me
– watch how I do it.

Learn the unforced rhythms of grace.
I will not lay anything heavy or ill-fitting on you.

Keep company with me,
and you will learn to live freely and lightly."

I cannot forgive myself or others

The spiritual need we are searching for here is Acceptance and Rest.

Matt 6 v 14 NIV

"For if you forgive other people
when they sin against you,
your Heavenly Father will forgive you."

Romans 8 v 33 TPT

"Who then would dare to accuse

those whom God has chosen
in love to be His?

God himself is the judge
who has issued his final verdict –
Not guilty! "

Romans 8 v 1 NIV

"Therefore,
there is now no condemnation
for those who are in Christ Jesus."

Micah 7 v 19 NLT

"Once again,
you will have compassion on us.
You will trample our sins under your feet
and throw them into the
depths of the ocean!"

I am alone

The spiritual need we are searching for here is Significance.

Joshua 1 v 9 NIV

"Be strong and courageous.
Do not be afraid; do not be discouraged,
for the Lord your God
will be with you
wherever you go."

Psalms 68 v 6 NLT

"God places the lonely in families.
He sets the prisoners free and gives them joy."

I am afraid

The spiritual need we are searching for here is Security.

1 John 4 v 18 NKJV

"Perfect love casts out all fear ".

2 Timothy 1 v 7 NKJV

"For God did not give us a spirit of fear,
but of power, love and a sound mind."

Isaiah 43 v 1 NKJV

"Fear not, for I have redeemed you;
I have called you by name.

You are Mine!"

I was recently in communion when a dear friend, who happened to be leading the congregation at the time, discussed the importance of our posture in prayer when we come to God.

She mentioned how we often come to God from a place of "I am not".

I am not good enough.
I am not worthy.
I am not lovable.
I am not capable.

Many of us consider this a humble and heavenly prayer, but when we look at the focus, who is it? It is *still* all about us.

We need to come to God with awe and honour because He is the great **"I AM"**, eyes fixed on His glory, not our deficiencies. He is trying to remind us to look up and focus on Him. Maybe if we come with a heavy heart, we might actually be coming with the spirit of "I am not good enough", God is saying, ***but*** **yet I AM.**

I am known as the **GREAT I AM** – look at me.

I AM good enough.
I AM worthy.
I AM loving.
I AM capable.

When we understand the true character of God, the Father, we can only come with awe. We want the loving Creator of everything to take control of our lives. We don't buy into the fallacy that we can control everything or, for that matter, anything. We surrender our lives to His will, not ours. We can trust He will meet our needs. He is truly Jehovah Jireh. We know He loves us from our first to our last breath and every breath in between. This is an important revelation because if we understand this, we can carry our rest.

Not choose to go to a place of rest, but **carry rest wherever we go.**

CHAPTER FIVE

Well of Life

We all know there are times when life can be incredibly difficult. Jesus creates a safe place for each of us to come. We don't need to fix our lives before spending time with him. He is interested and waiting at the well of refreshing right now to speak to you. I want to share another favourite story from the Bible. The story of the beautiful woman at the well. On its surface, the story records ethnic prejudice and a woman shunned by her community. But look deeper, and you'll realise it reveals a great deal about Jesus' character.

The story begins as Jesus and His disciples travel from Jerusalem in the south to Galilee in the north. To make their journey shorter, they take the quickest route, through Samaria. Tired and thirsty, Jesus sits by Jacob's well while His disciples go to the village of Sychar, roughly a half-mile away, to buy food. It is about noon, the hottest part of the day, when a Samaritan woman comes to the well to draw water.

At this moment, Jesus broke three Jewish customs. First, He spoke to this beautiful woman; this was not common for a male Jew. Second, she was a Samaritan, and the Jews traditionally despised Samaritans. Third, He asked her to get Him a drink of water, although using her cup or jar would have made Him ceremonially unclean.

Jesus' behaviour shocked the woman. But as if that weren't enough, He offered the woman "living water" as a gift from God so that she would never thirst again. Jesus used the words "living water" to refer to her spiritual needs, the gift that would satisfy her soul's desire:

John 4 v 11–18 NIV

'Sir,' the woman said,

'You have nothing to draw with
and the well is deep.
Where can you get this living water?
Are you greater than our Father Jacob,
who gave us the well
and drank from it himself,
as did also his sons and his livestock?'

Jesus answered,
'Everyone who drinks this water
will be thirsty again,
but whoever drinks the water

I give them will never thirst.

Indeed,
the water I give them
will become in them a spring of water
welling up to eternal life.'

The woman said to him,

'Sir, give me this water
so that I won't get thirsty and
have to keep coming here to draw water.'

He told her,
'Go, call your husband and come back.'

'I have no husband,'
she replied.

Jesus said to her,
'You are right when you say you have no husband.
The fact is, you have had five husbands,
and the man you now have is not your husband,
What you have just said is quite true.'

Jesus explains that living water is only available through Him. At first, the Samaritan woman does not fully understand Jesus. Although they had never met before, Jesus revealed that He knew she'd had five husbands and was now living with a man who was not her husband.

> "Sir, the woman said,
> you must be a prophet."

Jesus and the woman discussed their views on worship, and the woman voiced her belief that the Messiah was coming.

> Jesus declared,
> "I, the one speaking to you,
>
> **I am He."**

As the woman began to grasp the reality of her encounter with Jesus, the disciples returned. They, too, were shocked to find Jesus speaking to this woman. Leaving behind her water jar, the woman returned to town, inviting the people to "Come, see a man who told me all that I ever did."

This story is an absolute joy to read due to the subtle details and nuances within it.

The first detail is that Jesus is returning to Galilee. The exciting thing here is that He actively leads the disciples through Samaria. This was not the custom of the Jews, as they despised Samaritans and often travelled many miles around the land just so they wouldn't encounter anyone from this culture.

Not Jesus; He was making a beeline path for a beautiful, broken woman who needed God's refreshing.

To understand the hatred between the Jews and Samaritans, I will give you a quick history lesson. The feud between these two cultures was fierce and longstanding. In some ways, it dates back to the days of the patriarchs. Israel was divided into two kingdoms. The northern kingdom, Israel, established its capital first at Shechem and later at the hilltop city of Samaria, and the southern kingdom of Judah (Judea), their capital at Jerusalem.

In 722 BC; Assyria conquered Israel and took most of its people into captivity. These Assyrians brought with them their pagan idols, which the remaining Jews began to worship alongside the God of Israel, with intermarriages taking place. This is the beginning of the Samaritan culture. Meanwhile, the people of the southern kingdom of Judah were also carried off into captivity. But years later, a remnant of 43,000 Israelites was permitted to return and rebuild Jerusalem. The people who now inhabited the former northern kingdom, the Samaritans, tried to undermine the attempt to re-establish Jerusalem. So walls of bitterness were erected on both sides and did nothing but harden as the years followed.

When reading the Word, there are countless modern parallels between Jewish-Samaritan interactions and cultural discrimination today or wherever people are divided by racial and ethnic barriers. Perhaps that's why the Gospels and Acts provide so many instances of Samaritans coming into contact with the message of Jesus.

Anyway, getting back to Jesus, He travels with the disciples straight through the middle of Samaria and stops at the well, sending the disciples to get food. He already knows their preconceived and prejudiced ideas regarding this woman He is about to meet.

We also know the woman is coming to the well at noon. This is not customary for anyone, especially women of the day. They always collected water in groups in the early morning or late afternoon when it was cooler. Why would she do this? Well, let us look again at her story.

> Jesus said to her,
>
> "You are right when you say you have no husband.
> The fact is, you have had five husbands,
> and the man you now have is not your husband."

Here is a vulnerable woman who is not going to get her water in the early morning with the other women but draws her water at the hottest part of the day when no one comes to the well. It soon becomes obvious why she does, it is the safest time of the day from the gibes, jeers, and scorn of other women in her community.

She has had five husbands and now the man she is sharing her bed with is not her husband at all. You may have already made a judgement on her, maybe even through biblical patterns, but I ask you to reconsider these thoughts. The fact is, in the ancient world, there was a significant imbalance of power in the status between men and women, especially when it came to marriage. Divorce was easy for men but practically impossible for women. It may be that any of her husbands could have passed away, but it could also be a likely scenario that the issue was not a lack of morality but could have possibly been the ache of being unable to conceive a child.

Back in ancient times, having an heir was important, and if this did not sadly occur, it was considered an acceptable ground for divorce. As she had been married so many times; it does suggest she was incredibly beautiful and desirable, but the story may indicate some of these men decided later she was not fit for marriage and petitioned and granted divorce.

Let us presume that she did not necessarily choose these divorces, but they were thrust upon her. This is speculative, of course, but it is more likely than some of our previous misguided conceptions regarding morality. It was clear this woman had significantly suffered no matter the reasons, and Jesus saw it.

We know any woman or person travelling through the traumatic journey of divorce or being unable to conceive a child will experience feelings of loss, anxiety, deep profound sorrow, moments of fear and abandonment, and at times, loneliness.

If you are going through divorce, separation, or trying to conceive a child, I want to pray for you right now.

We pray to our God that sings over each of us,
We pray you will heal
the brokenhearted and hold this beautiful person's hand.

We ask that you remind us that our love,
worth and forgiveness can
all be found in you.

We know our minds can change and shift,
but you remain constant.

You are the true foundation we can
build our life on.

Your love is the same yesterday, today and forever.
We know that what we fail to understand,
you already know.

In the scramble to rearrange our lives,
you already see the purpose.

We pray for a true revelation that
you will never leave us alone, never forgotten.

We pray for resources when resources have been
lost, we pray for wisdom to walk with
grace and resilience.

We pray for endless energy;
all your power and all your love
to flood every inch of our life and body.

We pray for the revelation to see the beauty of
people and the love of the Father
so clearly, once again.

We stand on the promises that you will never leave
us, never walk away and never abandon us, Lord.

We know you go before us as our helper.
We know you will fight for us as our protector.

We know you always care and provide for us, and
we know you have a good future and plan for us.

In the name of Jesus Christ

Amen

In her society, we know the woman at the well would have been ostracised, and her life would have been incredibly difficult. Jesus creates a safe place for her to come. He sees her right where she is, in the middle of her messy life. He doesn't judge her. He knows her pain, just like He knows ours. Jesus thought she was worthy, worthy to walk into unfamiliar territory to pursue her. He made a direct path to her, just like He makes a direct path to you today.

He does not condemn her but shows He truly knows her and reminds her of her deepest spiritual needs. She is thirsty for the love of the Heavenly Father, searching in all the wrong places. She is seeking her spiritual needs of love, acceptance, significance, assurance, and security in relationships and in others who may not have truly understood her value or worth. She is giving up the most precious parts of herself for a sub-par existence, where she is humiliated, isolated, and degraded.

What I love is that one encounter with Jesus changes everything. She goes from isolating herself in the community, from feelings of shame and guilt, to publicly declaring the goodness of Jesus.

We all can internalise messages that we are not as strong, competent, and capable. We can unconsciously absorb beliefs about our rightful place in community, and those messages may present in how we judge each other and ourselves.

This thinking can lead us to mistreat, underestimate, and distance ourselves in order to feel protected from others. As women, I am sure most of us have, at some point, experienced being minimalised to such ridiculous values as how beautiful we are, how young we are, how slim we are, or how popular we are. It is so sad to see our community not recognise the amazing treasures we hold within.

We are all wonderfully and uniquely made by God, in different shapes and sizes, with different gifts and skills which we bring to our family, our community and to God. It is important to remember we were never designed to compete or compare, but uplift, empower, support and love each other.

It is important for all of us to look for our daughters, sons, partners, mums, dads, sisters, brothers and friends who may be at risk or trying to find their spiritual needs in others. Replacing God's authentic version for one that does not satisfy our thirst.

We need to be just like Jesus, not see the imperfections, lack, or loss, but see the person within. We need to encourage, include, stand alongside, and remind each other that we are beautiful and valuable in Jesus' eyes.

CHAPTER SIX

Asking God

In Luke 11, verse 5, we come across the story of the midnight friend. It begins like this:

"And Jesus said to them,

Which of you shall have a friend,
and go to him at midnight
and say to him,

Friend, lend me three loaves,
A friend of mine
has come to me on his journey,
and I have nothing to set before him.

And the Father
will answer from within and say,

'Do not trouble me; the door is now shut,

and **my children are with me in bed**;
I cannot rise and give to you!'

I say to you,
though he will not rise and give to him,

because he is his friend,
and because of his persistence,
he will rise and give him as many loaves as he needs."

When I read this verse, I always think of my beautiful friend, a single mum with nine children. She is an absolute superstar and passionately loves God and the Holy Spirit. In the first century, it was common for all the family to sleep in the same room. I can imagine her lying in that room with all her children, looking at the baby, hoping he would not wake from the noise of the banging neighbour outside. Let's continue to read this passage.

"So, I say to you, ask,
and it will be given to you;
seek, and you will find;
knock, and it will be opened to you.

For everyone who asks receives,
and he who seeks finds,
and to him who knocks, it will be opened.

If a son asks for bread
from any father among you,

will He give him a stone?

Or if he asks for a fish,
will He give him a serpent instead of a fish?

Or will he offer him a scorpion
if he asks for an egg?

If you, then, being evil,
know how to give good gifts to your children,

**How much more
will your Heavenly Father
give the Holy Spirit to those who ask Him!"**

As a long-term Christian, I had interpreted this passage as to ask and keep on asking, seek and keep on seeking, and knock and keep on knocking. I now have a new theory, which I would like to share with you. As I have read this passage more, I have also turned to the original text and translation. I have changed my thoughts regarding Jesus' true intention when teaching the disciples.

In first-century culture, it was considered the height of embarrassment or rudeness not to offer guests hospitality if they came to your home.

In ancient times, hospitality was not merely a question of good manners, but a moral virtue that grew out of the harsh desert and nomadic existence experienced by the people of Israel.

The biblical customs of welcoming the weary traveller and receiving the stranger were considered essential in Jewish culture. The Torah mentions the idea of "Welcoming the Stranger" no less than 36 times, and reinforces this idea by reminding the children of Israel that they were once strangers in a foreign land.

Bread was the essential, basic food for most Jews. It was so fundamental that in Hebrew, "to eat bread" and "to have a meal" are the same. Bread was respected, and many rules were created to preserve it. Any crumbs over the size of an olive were expected to be gathered and never discarded. Bread was never to be cut, but always broken.

In the story, the neighbour is caught unawares and discovers he has nothing to offer his friend. He goes to his neighbour, who is the Father in this story, to ask for bread. In this parable, I think most of us would agree that the Father in this story represents the Heavenly Father.

But my question to you is, where would you place yourself in the story? Who are you in this parable? I know personally, for many years, I considered myself the man begging for bread on the outside of the Father's home, but I want to challenge this thought. Could it be possible this is not us at all?

If we are children of God, where would we be situated – close to the Father? Let's look again: -

> "Do not trouble me;
> the door is now shut, and

> **my children are with me in bed;**
> I cannot rise and give to you?"

As a child of God, then where are you? Are you on the outside of the house knocking, or are you asleep with a full belly within the Father's home?

This concept is fundamental. Understanding God's **will** to provide for our needs can give us great comfort and rest in times of challenge and need.

This is confirmed in

Psalm 37 v 25 NLT

"Once, I was young, and now, I am old.
Yet I have never seen the godly abandoned
or **their children begging for bread."**

When we look at the original text it doesn't say - Ask and keep on asking, it simply says "Ask", It doesn't say, seek and keep on seeking; it says "Seek", and once again, it does not say knock and keep on knocking it says "Knock". I have considered many translations of this particular text - reading 44 with only four interpreting as continuing to ask. These four are paraphrased versions that don't always come from a direct translation of the original text.

So, what does this mean for us now? It means we need to consider our prayer life. Are we coming to God as the neighbour, the stranger, or His child? The clincher for me is the part where He says, "How much more will the Heavenly Father want to give the Holy Spirit to those that ask Him!"

Many years ago, I completely changed my prayer life. I went from approaching God as the stranger or the neighbour begging for his protection - to having a complete revelation of being His BELOVED child.

When you pray, how are you approaching God? If you are desperately praying over and over for the same outcome or starting your prayer with, "Please, please, God," can I suggest maybe you are praying like the neighbour? Changing your approach can transform your relationship with God. Can I recommend coming to Him from a place of gratefulness? The scriptures say we can enter His gates through thanksgiving and praise.

I usually start my prayer from a place of gratitude. Instead of "Please, God, protect my precious husband, children and grandchild", I come in holy reverence, thanking Him for *already* protecting my family and precious children.

Instead of praying, "Please God help my situation," I pray to the God who sings over me. I pray and trust His faithfulness, knowing that His goodness and mercy will follow me all the days of my life, and I will dwell in the house of the Lord forever. I often play worship music, sing, and pray in my Heavenly language so my Spirit joins Him, reminding me of who I am as **His BELOVED child.**

CHAPTER SEVEN

Be Bold

I am now nine and sitting in a Pentecostal Christian gathering in an old picture theatre. I am on the right balcony at the back, singing a psalm during communion. As we finished, the Pastor led us in prayer. That day had been like many before, attending church with my family. As I began to pray, my tongue started to change. At first, I was taken aback, but as I prayed further, I realised God was graciously filling me with His beautiful Heavenly language. The moment is clear, even 43 years later, my heart bursting with joy and crying with gratitude.

Being baptised in the Holy Spirit was not unknown in my young life. My parents and I attended a wonderful church, where being baptised by full immersion and receiving God's incredible power through His Holy Spirit was an essential part of our belief. Still, to this day, it is the most remarkable experience of my life.

For some of you reading this, what I am discussing may be foreign, or you may not be sure you want to experience God's Heavenly language at all. Can I gently encourage you to consider revisiting this promise of God, maybe read the early church in Acts afresh?

When we speak this beautiful language, our Spirit joins God's, and we begin to pray His will over our lives. What better way to live than through God's purpose?

We all know God dreams bigger for us than we can possibly imagine. He wants us to be His witnesses and to testify of His goodness.

Acts 1 v 8 NIV

Jesus says,
"But you will receive power,
when the Holy Spirit comes on you,
and you will be my witnesses in Jerusalem,
and in all Judea and Samaria,
and to the ends of the earth."

This means we have not just been called to live a life of self but to a life serving God and others. Being empowered by the Holy Spirit doesn't *just* mean speaking in tongues. It means so much more. He gives us the ability to step into God's purpose for our lives. Slowly by slowly, as we choose to follow Jesus, we will begin to become more like Him. The Holy Spirit will teach us. I love this passage of scripture as the Word describes the empowerment of the early church.

Acts 2 v 2 NIV

"When the day of Pentecost came,
they were all together in one place.
Suddenly, a sound like the blowing of
a violent wind came from heaven
and filled the whole house
where they were sitting.

They saw what seemed to be tongues of fire
that separated and came to rest on each of them.
All of them were filled with the Holy Spirit
and began to speak in other tongues
as the Spirit enabled them."

Later in that same chapter

"Peter replied,
"Repent and be baptised,
every one of you,
in the name of Jesus Christ
for the forgiveness of your sins.
And you will receive the gift of the Holy Spirit.

**The promise is for you
and your children
and for all who are far off—
for all whom the Lord our God will call."**

Over my many years of running Bible studies, I have seen time and time again when we seek God, we find Him. He has filled precious people to overflowing with His Holy Spirit, many who thought God's miraculous gift of His Heavenly language was not for them or relevant now.

I ask you again to come fresh to God with this request.

STOP right now, this very moment!

Get out of that comfy chair, put on some worship music and start praising our incredible Saviour.

I suggest speaking aloud and praying the highest form of praise to God – say Hallelujah, Hallelujah. His timing is perfect – don't get disheartened; continue to seek Him. His promises are yes and Amen, so continue to believe and pursue the Holy Spirit in all His glory.

CHAPTER EIGHT

Loving Others

Back in the mid-1980s, I was at a youth Christmas event. It was a fantastic opportunity to catch up with friends from other campuses. It was held in a small sporting facility in Adelaide at the Parks Community Centre.

There were many activities that night, and most were focused on sports. As you know from a previous chapter, I have no sporting abilities whatsoever, but as a young person, I would not miss this event for the world.

There was one thing that would pass on this night, thanks to my beautiful Mum. She kindly took my sister and I many a Saturday afternoon to the local roller-skating rink. Luckily, on this night, the large indoor stadium was transformed into a roller skating rink. I was in, I was good, and I was cool!

Now, I grew up in the craziest and most colourful decade of the last century. In the mid-80s, we wore big shoulder pads and parachute pants and had enormous hair – thanks to hairspray. There was teasing, scrunching and a beautiful flower-looking fringe, which was essential before you even thought of stepping outside your home. The words higher, the better, were often spoken regarding any hairstyle during this era. Looking back now, it was hideous, but I thought I was absolutely gorgeous.

If you are unsure what I am talking about or you did not have the privilege of growing up during this time, can I suggest stopping for a moment and google Jane Fonda in the 80s? It epitomised everything: the hair, the clothes, the multi-coloured eye shadow, and of course, my favourite blue opal silver-pink lipstick. Imagine a beautiful and fluorescent landscape with a distinct smell of hairspray as you read this part of the book, and you will be entirely on track.

So, to look my best, I would use nearly an entire can of hairspray when attending any important event. Many a family member has suggested that my teenage years consumption of spray cans may have single-handedly ruined the earth's ozone layer.

Unfortunately, most of these cans contained chlorofluorocarbons or CFCs. As a result, British scientists discovered the ozone hole in 1985. An international treaty, the Montréal Protocol, was created to protect the ozone layer by phasing out the production of numerous substances responsible for ozone depletion.

This could be why hair fashion was so sleek, slick, and flat in the 1990s. Even though I don't think I single-handedly destroyed the ozone layer, I will still take this moment to apologise to everyone reading this book.

So, there I was in all my glory, gliding on roller skates across the room, performing the over-the-leg crossover as I turned the corners when, from the side, this guy approached me. For young girls who have grown up in church, you know every available guy in this community. You have already ruled out some or decided all of them feel like brothers, not potential suitors, so I was surprised to meet someone I didn't know. He was a new Christian, and we started chatting. He told me how God had miraculously changed his life. He was so different from many of the boys I knew. He was very funny, which always gets us - doesn't it, girls? And had a fresh and new attitude regarding his faith.

We became friends immediately. Who could have imagined I would be meeting the love of my life that night, my husband, Joe, whom I am still married to 37 years later?

I remember my heart skipped a beat every time I met him. He had such depth and was kind, compassionate, and strong in his faith. I found I could talk to him for hours, which was a problem since the only phone in the house was in the kitchen underneath my father's gaze.

Over many conversations, he shared the story of his family and spoke of his grandparents in Europe during World War II. Unfortunately, his grandfather was captured by the

Nazis and taken to one of their notorious work camps in Poland. He suffered for many years. After the liberation, they left Germany and Poland to emigrate to Australia. Due to the trauma of the war, my husband's family found some solace in Australia, as well as in the drinking culture, to escape the memories and pain of the past.

This meant my husband's Mum grew up in a complex household with significant addictions, triggers and trauma. Unfortunately, this generational trauma was passed unintentionally to her. Sadly, my husband's Mum also began to lean on addiction to cope with the broken world she lived in, seeking all her spiritual needs in all the wrong places. She found herself with a heavy drug addiction, pregnant and unmarried in her late twenties.

In Australia during the 1960s, some young unmarried pregnant women left their homes or families to hide their condition from their community. When these women and girls needed the support of their families the most, they were isolated, lost and often abused. Many were taken advantage of and were "encouraged" to adopt their children to others. There are still women today facing the loss and consequences of society's unhelpful prejudices and unscrupulous adoption agencies, which forcibly remove babies from their mothers. Many of these poor girls returned home after a traumatic birth, losing their beautiful baby and then kept this unimaginable pain secret for years.

As a baby, my husband was fostered by a beautiful family who loved him dearly. Unfortunately, they needed to move interstate and were prohibited from taking him due to his mother's wishes. He was put up for adoption again, and this time, he was considered for kinship care and given to his grandparents. No matter how well-intentioned his grandparents were, the trauma of abuse continued.

When my husband was nine, his beautiful mother, who was still in the grips of a strong drug addiction, was tragically murdered. The family was again touched by horrific pain and sorrow. Understandably, his grandparents never recovered, turning deeper to alcohol to cope with the pain of losing their daughter.

Sadly, later, when my husband was thirteen, his grandfather suffered multiple strokes and unfortunately passed away before his eyes. His grandmother's mental health deteriorated; she became abusive, critical and violent.

At age fifteen, he walked out of the only home he ever knew with no direction or security. Only a few years later, he met God and experienced the Holy Spirit, which would drastically change his life.

I want to dedicate this chapter to him, his family and all the godly relationships of my life.

Our culture convinces us that friendship, marriage, and relationships are something **for** us rather than something **asked of** us.

We often approach people looking to fulfil our own spiritual needs, placing little emphasis on the vulnerable, traumatised or complex. We can find these people too difficult, but God has asked us to look again. How often do I meet people in church who are desperately searching to understand this life, to find a connection to God and others? Looking for love and acceptance in all the wrong places, struggling with addictions, negative identity messages, anxiety and depression.

When we think of relationships, we consider them an opportunity to bond two imperfect people. The difference is that through prayer, we invite the presence and wisdom of a perfect God into this union.

Understanding and valuing each other is important in this process. The revelation is we are all unique, valued, and designed by God. This understanding can help us find connection and real rest for our souls.

We all travel through life with different experiences. Unfortunately, sometimes, these experiences can be tragedy, trauma and abuse. This pain can quickly speak to our current circumstances and relationships.

We are all different and bring unique gifts to our lives, families, and communities. Knowing who we are helps us experience true freedom and understand our blind spots, strengths, and weaknesses. It sets us free not to compare or compete with others. It permits us to step into our authentic, most powerful selves and live a life of purpose and meaning. It also gives us the wisdom and grace to love others with the revelation of how important we each are to God.

LOVING OTHERS

Psalms 139 v 13-14 NIV

"For you created my innermost being,
you knit me together in my mother's womb.

I praise you because
I am fearfully and wonderfully made."

If you are anything like me, you love to observe people. As I did, I noticed anomalies in personalities and temperaments that I found very interesting. At the same time, I began studying personal discipleship through some of the teachings of Dr Ray Andrews from NewLife Worldwide Ministries.

One of my favourite teachers, a minister and psychologist, explains the concept of the unique temperament given by God. He discusses how we each bring a crucial, unique insight and perspective to our world.

As we grow, we encounter people who powerfully influence our lives and identities. Unfortunately, sometimes, this can be negative. It can profoundly impact how we engage with others or the community around us. It can stop us from living our authentic life, the abundant life Jesus spoke of in

John 10 v 10 NKJV

"The thief does not come except to steal,
and to kill and to destroy.
I have come that they may have life,

and that they may have it more abundantly."

We desperately seek others for love, significance, acceptance, security, and assurance, never finding rest. As our spiritual needs are not met, we turn to anything that will give us some comfort or relief — this can be through addictions, unhealthy relationships, people-pleasing, seeking wealth and status, and the search for endless knowledge. None of these coping mechanisms quench our thirst, which only God can fill.

The concept of these temperaments, or specific types of people, could be primarily grouped into the following baseline categories:

Thinker
Doer
Feeler

There is not one good temperament; they are all essential and desirable for life and society. This means every temperament is valuable in our community.

Understanding this concept can help us to be free and comfortable in our own skin. It teaches us to stop comparing ourselves to others. Let's examine these temperaments more closely.

You should find one or a combination that resonates with you.

You may also chuckle as you see your family and friends

described as we begin to uncover the beauty of our differences.

The Feeler Temperament

If you have a "Feeler" temperament, your deep emotional needs are approval, acceptance, attention, and social interaction. You love being around people, but you fear rejection, complex relationships, and pressuring people. You do not like living in a fixed or rigid environment.

You generally have many friends, are charismatic, and often bring colour to the world around you. Your strength is being able to talk to anyone, anywhere, anytime. You are caring, creative, empathetic, enthusiastic, motivational, personable, optimistic and relationship-focused.

Some of your weaknesses or struggles can be your insatiable need to feel accepted by people pleasing. You may feel quickly rejected and can become moody, weak-willed and irresponsible. You can sometimes be restless, fearful and competitive. You may find it challenging to concentrate and can be impulsive.

Your charisma and free-loving nature can often attract people, which can lead to turning to unhealthy relationships for your spiritual needs.

Your energy levels are low at the beginning of the day, moderate by midday and high in the evening. You need plenty of time with others, and quality time with others is essential.

Spiritual

You feel God before you believe God, and you can often want to run away from God when you fail. You are sensitive to others' feelings and have an incredible ability to encourage and embrace grace. God created you for evangelism, encouragement, and merciful caring.

The Thinker Temperament

If you have a "Thinker" temperament, your deep emotional need is to be understood; you value truth, security, verbal acceptance, and time alone. You have 1-3 close friends who are incredibly loyal. You don't have high social needs and often enjoy being at home.

You can often see things as black and white, love lists, weigh your words carefully and always have something on your mind. You are generally the most moral temperament, pay attention to detail, dislike change, love rules and boundaries and like to be in control of your own space.

Some of your strengths are that you are incredibly loyal, love detail and order, are logical, gifted, self-sacrificing, faithful, committed, and often philosophical. You think over things carefully; you like recognition, need time to adjust before you act and need quiet time alone, as people can drain your energy. Your energy level is maximum at the start of the day and decreases as the day goes on.

One of your most significant spiritual barriers can be unbelief. You can become obsessive, critical, prideful, perfectionistic, negative, unwilling to take risks, occasionally rigid and controlled by guilt. You can be predisposed to anxiety or depression. You can find it very difficult to forgive others or let things go.

Spiritual

Hearing from God comes from theological insight. God created you as great disciplers, good teachers and great administrators in the community.

The Doer Temperament

If you have a "Doer" temperament, your deep emotional need is recognition. You like challenges and goals, unrestricted boundaries, and being in control. You will initiate social interaction and can be charming, outgoing, and inspiring. You are strong-willed, cannot see obstacles, and have an outcome focus.

You project confidence and independence, get quickly bored, hate to be confused by the facts and do not like imposed rules. You are assertive, fearless, efficient, independent and self-motivated. You are not easily discouraged and are quick to move into action.

You are high in energy, which is consistent throughout the day.

Your weakness is your pride. You can be insensitive, controlling, impatient, and demanding, sometimes arrogant and sarcastic, and have little tolerance for perceived weakness.

Spiritual

You desire and respect God's power. God created you as excellent leaders and church planters. You are also great at initiating change and becoming drivers of faith and movement.

The Multifaceted Temperament

This temperament is an equal mix of all three temperaments and happens to be mine.

You value a peaceful environment and appreciate security and verbal acceptance. You are warm, safe, well-rounded, and flexible. You enjoy people; however, you need to be alone to rejuvenate. You have the best mind for ideas, are dreamers and can look at things from several different angles.

You fear the loss of security or being controlled by others. You are friendly, realistic, very connected to your children, conservative, and do not control others. You avoid conflict and keep the peace at all costs.

You have moderate energy levels consistent throughout the day.

You are dependable, very independent, hardworking, and a collaborator. You are also kind-hearted, sympathetic, and have an eye for injustice.

Your weaknesses include being self-righteous, stubborn, selfish, unmotivated, cynical, and worried.

Spiritual

You are great peacemakers and can adapt and serve in many different positions within the church environment.

Hopefully, you may have resonated with at least one or a combination of these descriptors. This insight may help you to recognise and value different temperaments in your current relationships. Stopping to understand others can help maintain healthy relationships and genuinely love others. It allows us to see each person as God sees them and love them as God loves them.

This provides perspective and an opportunity to view the world through someone else's eyes. We begin to value our differences as we see how God perfectly designed our husband, friend, child, or colleague to complement our strengths and weaknesses. His way to build a perfect picture, part of an ideal whole. Valuing others and their gifts helps us to be more considerate, kind, patient and caring.

We can identify and celebrate areas of strength and give grace to areas of vulnerability. We quickly move through conflict and work to resolve issues respectfully and helpfully.

We are called to love others, and I pray this chapter will help you to do so in a new and fresh way. Remember, when we come together as one, joys are multiplied, and sorrows are divided.

In Ephesians 4 v 16 NLT

"He makes the whole body fit together perfectly.
As each part does its own special work,
it helps the other parts grow,
so that the whole body
is healthy and growing and full of love."

Martin Luther King Jr prophetically wrote from prison about the problem and responsibility of the division of people. He called us not just to be a tail light, shining a light on what went wrong, but a headlight, shining a light on what could be. Grace prepares us in relationships with others, but wisdom launches those relationships forward, so let's be wise, tolerant and kind as we move through this beautiful life together.

CHAPTER NINE

The Embrace

Ephesians 4 v 20 TPT

"Never doubt God's mighty power
to work in you and accomplish all this.
He will achieve infinitely more
than your greatest request,
your most unbelievable dream,
and exceed your wildest imagination.

He will outdo them all for his miraculous
power constantly energises you."

In 2005, we moved from a small villa home to a large old house in Happy Valley, built in 1840. I remember the first day my husband and I saw it. It was charming, with multiple chimneys, a cellar, three bathrooms, and lots of rambling bedrooms. It was perfect.

We had considered our little three-bedroom home was getting too small. I was inclined to invite friends who were going through difficult periods to come and stay with us in the hope of healing. So, I was looking to find a house big enough to support many people, as many as God indicated.

You may be wondering what my beautiful husband was thinking regarding this extravagant plan, but he agreed. He had experienced homelessness as a teenager and understood the complexity of family trauma, so we put in an offer. It was soon accepted, and we began one of the happiest times of our lives, loving God and practically loving people.

It was a great place to heal, share a meal and do life together. For over 15 years, we laughed, lived and loved others, but slowly, as our lives changed, I believed God was calling us to do more. I discussed this with my husband.

At the time, we attended a beautiful conservative church. I knew my amazing God was there, but I strangely felt this crushing weight which I could not explain. Of course, I saw some people flourish in this space, the structured, the rule followers, the doers, and thinkers, but then I saw equally other people struggle through the unrelenting expectations of others. It was always the same sort of person: the creatives, the unstructured, the free thinkers, the sensitive ones. I loved these people, and seeing them fall under the weight of expectation and faith to conform broke my heart.

I knew God had created all of us and that we were dear and valued by Him. I was seeing a cookie-cutter version of Christianity, and if you did not fit that shape, there was a significant risk of getting lost along the way. My heart grieved.

As I travelled down this path, one of my children was struggling. I watched their beautiful little light start to dim. I learnt the importance of supporting and encouraging someone when in crisis and the trauma it caused when they were isolated.

It came to a critical point where I saw a dear friend attempt to take his life. He described the crushing pressure and expectation of his belief in himself and God and decided to leave.

I wanted to help everyone feel safe in church, to belong, not to be fearful of complex needs or messy lives, but to bring them all to the feet of Jesus. These people captured my heart.

I want to share one of my favourite passages in the Bible, the story of the prodigal son.

The parable begins with a man who has two sons, and the younger of them asks his Father to give him his share of the estate.

The implication is the son did not want to wait for his Father's death for his inheritance but instead wanted it immediately. This was an incredible insult to the Father, but he agreed and divided his estate between the two sons.

Upon receiving his portion of the inheritance, the younger son travels to a distant country, where he indulges in extravagant living. It is not long, however, before he is exhausted and has used all his Father's money.

A permanent drought strikes the land, and this leaves him desperately poor. He is forced to sell his possessions to pay his debts. Unfortunately, starving, he can only take work looking after pigs. He reaches the point of envying the food of the pigs that he is tending to. Only at this time does he finally recognise the value of his family and the stability of his home.

The Word declares:

> "And when he came to himself,
> he said,
> 'How many hired servants of my Fathers
> have bread enough and to spare,
> and I perish with hunger!
>
> I will arise and go to my Father
> and will say unto him,
> Father, I have sinned against heaven,
> and before you,
>
> and I am no more worthy to be called your son:
> make me as one of thy hired servants."

From his statement, it is interesting that the son is still focused on his own needs, not on loving or wanting to restore a relationship with his Father. How often do we approach the Heavenly Father from this perspective? From a place of need, not for the incredible relationship He is offering.

The prodigal son also didn't believe he was worthy to be received as a son because of his behaviour and sin to the Father. What is truly remarkable is the Father's response in this story; it is genuinely heart-warming.

> "And he arose and came to his Father
> but when he was yet a great way off,
>
> **(I love this next bit)**
>
> His father saw him,
> and had compassion, and RAN,
>
> and fell on his neck and kissed him."

Did you read that – **He ran to his son!!!**

Just like the Heavenly Father runs to us, the first moment He sees us trying to make our way back to Him. I love this part because it states the Father's heart, but it also incredibly states the heart of our Heavenly Father.

This implies that the Father was waiting at the gate, watching, hoping for the son's return, just as God is waiting for you.

The son starts his rehearsed speech, admitting his sins and declaring himself unworthy. Still, in most versions of Luke, the son does not even finish before his Father accepts him wholeheartedly without hesitation.

The Father calls for his servants to dress the son in the finest robe available, get a ring for his finger and sandals for his feet, and slaughter the calf for a celebratory meal.

In my own life, I remember I had spent many a day and night crushed by the loss of connection to my child after conflict meant we could no longer peacefully live in the same space.

I ached for their presence and would close their empty bedroom door to just relieve the pain. I remembered in tears, in years past, as I had argued with them about all sorts of things, some trivial like cleaning up their room. Now, I had a spotlessly clean room, and I ached for the messy one with them in it. Seeing the state of this perfectly ordered space felt like an arrow to my already wounded heart and made their missing presence in my life profound.

I ached to solve our previous disagreements and wanted to mend their heartache. I was overwhelmed with shame for not being good enough and for not finding the right words to say. I couldn't help but wonder how I could ever bridge the gap that had formed in our hearts. If only I could fix this or if only I could do better.

I remember sitting in life, looking at other people and their perceived happy families, wondering what they had done so right and what I had done so incredibly wrong.

My children were my life. They were **my identity**. I felt like I was failing in this area, which was heartbreaking and completely soul-destroying. Somehow, I had allowed them to fill my spiritual needs for love, acceptance, and significance. I remember silently crying in my bed early on Saturday night. I wished I had the wisdom to know how to reach them. I tried to approach them in the ways I thought were best, but we couldn't seem to find a safe emotional space to discuss our hurts and emotional differences.

My husband entered the darkened room and whispered, "Are you okay?" I said quietly, "Not really." He hugged me tightly and said, "You are a good Mum, and you know that God loves both our children even more than you do! He added, I know you think, is that even possible? But I assure you He does. Trust him, He doesn't sleep. He is working 24/7 to bring them home to you."

At that moment, my husband did something profound and amazing. He stopped me in the middle of my pain and sorrow and released me from the guilt, the crushing responsibility to fix everything. He gave me room to feel sad but sat alongside me to hold my pain. He reminded me of my identity and the identity of my children and gave me hope.

One glorious day, after God did amazing work in both our lives, my child decided to return home. I could not believe it, my heart's desire. I could hear them quietly praying as I walked down the hallway past their bedroom door. I stood in the hallway feeling like my heart was going to burst. I was so grateful to God for His mercy and goodness. I remember saying "thank you" silently, not wanting to disturb their time with God, and for bringing my precious child home.

After I thanked God, the Holy Spirit prompted me and said, "But who is bringing my sons and daughters home?"

I remember thinking - I am not sure I can bring vulnerable or traumatised people into my church. I was unsure if it was emotionally safe. I remembered my friend, their actions and thoughts on God and His supposed expectations for them. My church was loving but struggled with new people who had significant trauma or pain and Christians who may have made significant mistakes in their lives.

I remember as clear as day I heard the words: "Move On".

What did this mean? To give you context, I was a part of this wonderful congregation for over forty years. It was my family, my everything. The gravity of this decision meant leaving everyone I ever knew, my family and my friends. Due to the exclusive nature of the church and unresolved fear, many of the congregation would be unable to understand my decision.

Unfortunately, in the past, this community had encouraged people not to socialise with anyone who decided to leave. This meant the real risk of losing long-term friends, maybe family, and my comfortable Christian life.

My whole life was wrapped up in this community. The question kept running through my mind "Was I willing to give up my comfort, my familiarity, my family, my safety and security to follow God's calling?" The answer could only be yes; how could I say no?

I now fully understood the pain and trauma of losing connection with my child. How could I stand by and watch God suffer the same pain when He had graciously healed my heart and restored my precious relationship?

Following Jesus and his example was important in every area of my life but now it seemed even more so. I knew the devastating impact of pain, trauma, and wrong identity messages and how this could influence relationships and faith.

I wanted to find a community that was kind of heart and had love and true compassion for all people. It was important to me to find a church that was Bible-based and showed the heart of the Father. I wanted a church that represented different ages, diverse cultures, and life experiences—a place where even the most complex in our society felt safe to belong and would be included. Most importantly, I wanted people to find the gracious love of the Heavenly Father. What a shopping list! Not much to ask, right? I knew there wasn't a perfect church, but I would try to find something close.

I would like to take a moment to acknowledge some of the most amazing members of my past congregation who have spoken over me historically and those who continue to have the courage to speak over me now. I love all of you very much.

I know God has different plans for us all, but I want to encourage you not to be fearful of the mess or differences of others. When we come together, the body starts to heal and become whole. We are all important to God. If you are willing to listen, the Holy Spirit will guide you in speaking and encouraging others. I trust God's path, knowing He calls all of us to different parts of the same vineyard but for the same purpose. We do not need to be divided, we are so much stronger together.

So, this began the great church adventure. As we visited churches in the area, I held tightly to my old King James Bible, determined to find a bible-based church with a genuinely kind and loving heart. We began to experience all the differences of Christianity; some churches were very free, and some were even more conservative.

Women served in significant roles in the church, something I was unfamiliar with. I remember seeing a woman serving communion—this was wonderful. The men of my previous church had always conducted all these roles. I also saw women preachers and women serving and supporting in pastoral care. It opened my eyes to the wisdom of women pastorally caring for women. This gave me incredible opportunities to serve my Heavenly Father in a completely new way.

I knew that I was not given a female version of the Holy Spirit but a powerful and truly wonderful gift from God, which I needed to honour in all His glory. I read scriptures that supported women's presence in these spaces, like Deborah, Pheobe, Miriam, Rahab, Esther, Huldah, Mary Magdalene, Mary of Bethany, Lydia, Priscilla and many more.

Joel 2 v 28 speaks of a time when God would pour out his Spirit on all flesh: "Your sons and daughters will prophesy". On the Day of Pentecost, Peter confirmed the time had come, which is still true today! Any son or daughter of God has the full rights and privilege to declare His word, testify to His salvation, and prophesy by His Spirit.

I devoured books regarding the importance of women in our church and the opportunities for women's ministry. I travelled to Israel and studied the Word. I dipped in the Jordan River, sat on the banks of the Sea of Galilee, went to Jerusalem, to the Mount of Olives, stood at the Western Wall and prayed. It was exhilarating. I could not get enough of the Word and the connections between the Old and New Testaments. I found myself standing in the ancient archaeological dig of the city of Magdala, the hometown of Mary Magdalene, looking at the mosaic floor of the old synagogue and a place where Jesus was believed to have taught.

I love the story of Mary of Magdala or Magdalene because we know she was much like the woman I encountered on the beach in chapter one.

She had lived a life traumatised by her mental health, abused by her community and ostracised by her family. The Bible describes in detail her suffering and life, struggling through significant mental health challenges.

She had one encounter with Jesus, and everything changed. She came to the feet of Jesus, and her life was completely turned around. I have a beautiful friend who is also a Christian psychologist. She faithfully speaks:

> **"There is nothing that coming
> to the feet of Jesus cannot heal."**

Mary was among the few disciples who dared to support Jesus at the crucifixion. She knew what it felt like to be isolated, to suffer and to be ostracised in the community.

I believe God sometimes allows us some emotional scars to give us the wisdom, authority and compassion to speak and support others in times of trauma and pain.

I don't think we can truly imagine how horrific the crucifixion would have been, yet Mary stood through it all as a support to Jesus and His earthly family.

As we see, even after Christ's death and before his resurrection, she was still incredibly dedicated to loving and serving Him.

In Luke 24 v 1- 11 NIV

"On the first day of the week,
early in the morning, the women took the spices
they had prepared and went to the tomb.

They found the stone rolled away from the tomb,
but when they entered,
they did not find the body of the Lord Jesus.

While they were wondering about this,
suddenly two men in clothes that gleamed like lightning

stood beside them.

In their fright, the women bowed down with their faces to the ground, but the men said to them,

'Why do you look for the living among the dead?
He is not here; he has risen!

Remember how he told you,
while he was still with you in Galilee:
The Son of Man must be delivered
over to the hands of sinners,
be crucified and on the third day,
be raised again.'

Then they remembered His words.

When they came back from the tomb,
they told all these things to the eleven
and all the others.

It was

Mary Magdalene,

Joanna, Mary, the mother of James,

and the others with them
who told this to the apostles."

What a fantastic thought! God had given the most privileged gift to Mary and the other women, to be the first people to witness and declare Jesus's resurrection and proclaim the first gospel that He was risen. What an honour. A beautiful woman, abused, labelled, isolated, ostracised and chosen for her faith, consistent dedication and courage to preach the good news.

Scripture tells us the other disciples were hiding in a locked room. They had gathered together, but fearful of the Jews, they had locked all the doors in the house. In Luke's version, Jesus materialised in front of them while they were hiding, which scares them even more. I am sure Jesus might have written a future note to self – do not materialise in front of scared people, even if you can.

Even Saul was blinded many years later when Jesus called to him. I wondered how long Jesus knocked on the outside of the door that day before He decided He would have to go in the heavenly way. I cannot help but love a little sneaky ninja Jesus!

I wonder if He is also knocking on the door of your heart today, and you might be too afraid to answer. Shame and trauma can do this. They can make you put a wall around your heart to protect it, which only places you in a prison of disconnection, pain, and loneliness. I encourage you; it is truly time to break free.

Remember, we are never too broken, too messy and too lonely to come to Jesus. Mary is the perfect example of this. So, don't rule yourself out because:

Psalms 68 v 6 NLT

God places the lonely in families;
he sets the prisoners free and gives them joy."

Psalms 34:18 NIV

"The LORD is near to the broken-hearted
and saves the crushed in spirit."

It is time to break open that emotional prison, a prison of disconnection, of shame or guilt and give God a chance to heal your heart.

He is calling you to connect to church community or begin reading His love letter from home. Come and spend time with him. He is gentle and kind, so let him heal you completely.

Look for His freely and lightly. I am confident He will show you the way.

He is waiting at the gate, waiting to run

waiting to embrace you.

CHAPTER TEN

Dream Life

I began holding regular ladies' gatherings as an opportunity to bring women together. You did not need to attend church to come, and you did not even need to have faith in God. I would simply open my house and put the kettle on.

I would typically send an open text a few days before, inviting all the women I knew for a cuppa to talk about our amazing Saviour.

My text would read:

"Hey, gorgeous girl,
Are you tired, weary and heavy-laden,
looking for refreshment?
Bring your mothers, daughters,
and friends to my house,
Friday night to eat cheese, chocolate, drink coffee
and talk about our amazing Saviour."

I had no restrictions; all ages were welcome. Women attended, even hearing through other Christian communities. I learnt to trust God and be excited to see who He would send across my door for the evening.

I valued this space as precious and spent hours with God in prayer and His Word, asking His heart to be upon every girl attending. I watched as the Holy Spirit ministered across the room to many women who were lonely, suffering, isolated and those who might be stuck in their faith.

I watched women love the opportunity to talk about their lives, encourage others and share their pain. I saw women empathise, grow in their faith and receive the Holy Spirit. It became my joy and my life.

In fact, as my husband and I travelled through the Middle East, our guide took us to Nazareth, where this vast Catholic church pays homage to the mother of Jesus, Mary. It is a magnificent building with tributes on its walls from around the world, including Australia. Our guide, asked if he could take us to his favourite place, in Nazareth. We followed him through this back area, through an old market, to a tiny little wooden door. On the other side was this old first-century synagogue, believed to be the very one in which Jesus had started His ministry after the forty-day fast and temptation in the wilderness.

Luke 4 v 16-19 NIV

"He went to Nazareth,
where he had been brought up,
and on the Sabbath day,
he went into the synagogue,
as was the custom.

He stood up to read,
and the scroll of the
prophet Isaiah was handed to him.

Unrolling it, he found
the place where it was written:
"The Spirit of the Lord is on me
because he has anointed me to proclaim good news
to the poor.
He has sent me to proclaim freedom
for the prisoners
and recovery of sight for the blind,
to set the oppressed free,
to proclaim the year of the Lord's favour."

I sat on an old wooden bench in this ancient, stone-walled, arched building, I opened my Bible, and read this verse, thinking about my calling. As I began to support new people and women's ministry, I saw God's revelation of His purpose for my life. It became my calling.

I underwent a transformation in my faith, from Guilt to

Grace to Gratitude. I redefined my relationship with God and my understanding of theology – simple statements like these became profound in my life.

GUILT forces us to see our sin
GRACE forgives and removes our sin.

GUILT accuses us
GRACE equips and empowers us

GUILT causes fear
GRACE produces faith!

GUILT says there is something you *have* to do
GRACE says there is something we *get* to do!

Encountering the love and grace of Jesus changed everything. Instead of being stuck in a focus of my guilt and shame, I embraced His love and grace, which couldn't help but produce gratitude.

Many people don't ever travel down this path, stuck in a place of guilt or despair, but that is not God's plan for you. He wants us to step towards grace, have a true revelation of His love, and begin a life of gratitude—a life of living, giving, and loving others.

We organised groups to travel to interstate women's conferences, supporting women financially so they could afford to come. We prayed for women to encounter the baptism of the Holy Spirit. We started practical ministries - through a beautiful woman who worked at a Bakery close to my home. She asked her manager if she could collect the leftover bread, which was being thrown at the end of the day, and give it to some of the single mums we knew. But, of course, when we worship the God of abundance, we receive baskets of bread that could feed not only the women in our group but many other vulnerable families in our church and community. This ministry still runs today.

We saw women grow in their faith, isolated women find connection, as we found practical ways to pull our resources to support each other.

I connected with another lovely woman in church who faithfully ran a knitting ministry. She would sit with a group of women chatting, praying and worshipping as they knitted the most beautiful, colourful and special patchwork blankets.

As I write this book, I sit with one of these most beautiful creations on my lap. We began blessing these to friends and family members suffering in hospital and the community, explaining the prayerful love and care of each one's creation. We watched as people's eyes glistened as they heard of the women who prayed and sang for them. As I prayed and visited terminally ill patients, I watched them clutch their blankets, feeling the love of the Father as it sat lovingly on their laps. Nurses ask about these colourful additions to their beds. This enabled the gift of love and testimony to spread even further.

I recalled reading this passage in the Word which is so very true.

Proverbs 11 v 24 MSG
"The world of the generous gets larger and larger."

I saw women encouraging each other to look for *their* giftings and additional resources, believing and knowing God had faithfully placed in each of their hearts and hands. This gave them permission and courage to love others in a way that was unique and specifically relevant to them.

To help you today, I have placed a questionnaire at the end of this chapter to help identify your gifts.

To this day, I continue to be passionate about connection, new people's ministry and the encouragement of women.

We still see new women come to faith and prodigals return home, all encountering God and a community that specifically carries the fragrance of Jesus. I stopped living a life with an inward focus and fixed my eyes on God. His love gave me the capacity and courage to love others, just like Jesus did. I stopped looking at my imperfections, of which there are many and trusted God to give me all I required to step into His purpose and destiny for my life. God's love overflowed as I found joy, peace, patience, kindness, gentleness, faithfulness and rest.

There was only one problem. I could not fit all the women who wanted to attend the ladies' group in my home. I prayed and approached my husband, telling him of my crazy idea. What about we move from our "Dream house to our Dream life!" We had always wanted to live by the ocean, and if we could find a simple house with one large area to accommodate a women's gathering, it would be wonderful. He had watched as I slowly gained confidence in this area. He knew my commitment to invest in, loving, and encouraging the girls.

Simultaneously, I had been toying with a more minimalistic life to create capacity and clarity and find ways to enjoy and serve God effectively.

My current home was great, but our children were growing older, and I wanted to simplify our lives by spending more time doing the things we loved together:

I had four goals:

1. I wanted to find a small home with a big heart. By this, I meant a flexible house with one spacious room. I still wanted my large dining table to entertain and lots of room to hold women's gatherings, but I didn't need much more than a bedroom and bathroom.

2. Reduce my debt so I could work less and be truly financially free.

3. I wanted to reduce space, remove clutter, and keep only things that were practical for my day-to-day life and that brought me joy.

4. Find a way to save time, to create more opportunities for fun and for the people I love.

And one little deep heart's desire – a towel walk to the ocean, and if possible, any sea view, even if I had to stand on the toilet seat to see it!

While we searched, we went through many homes that were a little out of our budget, but finally, we found one that fit most of our needs. I was excited as we were finally going to make an offer.

Being the excitable woman I am, we left our home way too early and had 40 minutes to spare before the open inspection appointment time began. On the way, we saw a property inspection sign in an area we had not considered, so we decided to use up some of this time and go and have a look.

As we drove down the road, we moved closer and closer to the waves and the ocean. Eventually, we went over the top of this hill, and there was a view of endless miles of ocean and this little house for open inspection.

As we entered the house, I immediately ran upstairs to the second level to see the view. There was a big open room, big enough for many women to gather.

I remember my husband giving me the look like 'Stay cool' and telling me not to give anything away to the real estate agent. I looked at the view and imagined the beautiful life I would lead, the women's groups, the old velvet chair, and the prayer sessions with God. A tear rolled down my cheek as my husband smiled, and I knew we were home.

If you are new to faith, you might want to revisit this section a little later. If you attend a church community, you might like to take a moment to fill out this simple Spiritual Gifts Survey. From my experience, one of the easiest ways to find true joy is to start loving and serving others.

Understanding who you are and how you are designed gives you the opportunity to serve from a place of ease and lightness.

Spiritual Gifts Survey

Ephesians 4 v 16 NLT
"He makes the whole body fit together perfectly.
As each part does its special work,
it helps the other parts grow,
that the whole body is healthy
and growing in full of love."

"We all have different gifts,
according to the grace given to each of us.

If your gift is **prophesying**, then prophesy in accordance with your faith,

if it is **serving**, then serve;
if it is **teaching**, then teach;

if it is to **encourage**; then encourage,
if it is **giving**, then give generously,

if it is to **lead**, do it diligently,

if it is to show **mercy**, do it cheerfully."

Let us discuss these gifts in more detail.

Prophecy

The gift of prophecy is about applying God's mind to our life situations. It is speaking God's 'now' word to strengthen, encourage, and comfort others. It is sharing what God, the Holy Spirit, has revealed. Those with this gift are confident, knowing the scriptures are the source of all truth. They are teachable and have a deep capacity to trust God.

Serving

The gift of serving builds and mobilises the Church by meeting practical needs and performing the necessary functions that make the community of faith effective. People with this gift are humble and available; they love to bless others through practical, hands-on help.

Teaching

This gift lets one break down scripture and clearly explain its meaning to others. A person with a teaching gift is passionate about the truth of God's word and how it can be understood and applied in people's lives. These people study the scriptures diligently and motivate others to do the same.

Encouragement

The gift of encouragement inspires and motivates people to live life to their full potential in Christ. A person with this gift is motivated to see believers mature in Christ and grow spiritually. They are willing and eager to come alongside and encourage others through all situations and circumstances of life. They love to remind people of the personal promises of God.

Giving

The gift of motivated and generous giving contributes resources to meet kingdom needs. It is about unapologetic spiritual generosity—the ability to joyfully give finances and tangible resources to meet the needs of others and support the ministry of the Gospel. People with this gift see the resources that God has given them as something to steward and manage with wisdom.

Leadership/Organisation

People with the gift of leadership are organised and can see what needs to be done to mobilise others to achieve God's vision. They can break down large jobs into simple steps that others can easily engage in. As organisers, they can motivate with clarity, solve problems, and delegate effectively. These people often can create systems and processes that support the vision.

Mercy

The gift of mercy is the capacity to care for and see healing in the lives of vulnerable people God deeply loves. This empathetic heart reaches out to those who currently can't care for themselves. These people have God-given compassion and love to see others come to spiritual and emotional wholeness.

Spiritual Gift Survey Instructions

A list of statements has been prepared below to help you discover your spiritual gifting.

Read each statement and then rate yourself using this number system below.

3 = **Always**
2 = **Sometimes**
1 = **Hardly at all**
0 = **Not at all**

Add the scores from each statement for each gift and write in the total at the end of every section. The highest totals are a good indication of your motivational gifts. You may have more than one.

Note * Score yourself based on what currently fulfils and satisfies you rather than what you would *like* to be. Be honest and be yourself. God has created us all uniquely, and we are all celebrated and needed in our church family.

QUESTIONNAIRE

Section 1

1. I like praying and interceding for people so that I can share thoughts that will encourage and strengthen others.

2. I often have a strong sense of what God wants to say to individuals or groups of people.

3. I have a strong sense of right and wrong, and I am prepared to speak God's truth regardless of whether others agree.

4. I can often discern dishonesty or deception in the motives or actions of others.

5. I find it relatively easy to sense precisely what God wants to do in a church meeting.

PROPHECY   **TOTAL:**

Section 2

1. I enjoy getting together with people to help with church projects and teams.

2. I enjoy doing practical, behind-the-scenes work, especially if it allows other leaders to focus on the task God has specifically called them to.

3. I am happy to work on any task, even when that task is not noticed or acknowledged.

4. I can see the practical needs that others don't see.

5. I am very dependable for getting things done.

GIFTING – Serving   **TOTAL:**

Section 3

1. I love explaining biblical truth in a way that people can clearly understand.

2. I enjoy studying the Bible, researching a subject and sharing what I learn with others.

3. I am concerned that Biblical truth should be represented clearly, logically, and balanced, with proper attention to the meaning of words, so that it will be understood correctly.

4. I am diligent in my daily study of the Bible and

desire to gain as much knowledge as I can.

5. I can make the Bible clear and relevant to others.

TEACHING **TOTAL:**

Section 4

1. People often come to me with their personal challenges for my input.

2. I enjoy encouraging those who are discouraged and downhearted.

3. I get great pleasure from motivating people to have a vision for their spiritual lives and reach their potential in Christ.

4. I like to show others how difficulties and trials can be opportunities for spiritual growth.

5. I encourage others to draw closer to God's love when they face challenges or disappointment.

ENCOURAGEMENT **TOTAL:**

Section 5

1. I like managing my money efficiently to give generously to the kingdom of God.

2. I cheerfully give more than regular tithes because

I love to see the things of God move forward in practical ways.

3. I have no problem in joyfully entrusting my assets to others for the work of the Gospel.

4. I often give anonymously to those in need.

5. I am willing to sacrifice and go without to provide the funds required for the work of the kingdom of God.

GIVING   **TOTAL:**

Section 6

1. I enjoy planning tasks for others and supplying them with the details to engage efficiently and easily.

2. I can visualise the result of a project and like to organise teams and resources to accomplish the goal.

3. I am very conscious of the importance of efficient administration so that every aspect of a project runs smoothly.

4. I will step in and make things happen in a group without a leader.

5. I can break down an enormous task into smaller achievable goals and then delegate those smaller

parts to others.

LEADERSHIP   **TOTAL:**

Section 7

1. I have a tender heart toward the vulnerable and often do what I can to help those in distress.

2. I enjoy visiting those who are lonely in the hospital or having a hard time.

3. I tend to look out for those who are neglected or alienated.

4. I work happily with those who are ignored by the majority and find myself naturally drawn to these people.

5. I can relate to others who are emotionally hurting and gain satisfaction from being able to help them.

MERCY   **TOTAL:**

As I mentioned before – read each statement and then rate yourself using this number system below.

3 = **Always**
2 = **Sometimes**
1 = **Hardly at all**
0 = **Not at all**

Add the scores from each statement for each gift and write in the total.

The highest totals are a good indication of your spiritual and motivational gifts. You may have more than one.

When you know and understand the **gifts** God has given to you personally and activate them in your life, you will discover a renewed sense of purpose and excitement. You will partner **with** God to love the people around you in fresh and new ways.

Why don't you complete the survey, step out in faith, and begin to serve God in your unique God shape? I genuinely believe this is where the **joy of life** is found.

Trust Him He will lead the way.

CHAPTER ELEVEN

Are You Worried

Luke 10 v 38–42 NIV

"As Jesus and his disciples were on their way,
he came to a village where a woman named
Martha opened her home to him".
She had a sister called Mary,
who sat at the Lord's feet, listening to what he said.

But Martha was distracted by all the preparations that had
to be made.
She came to him and asked,
'Lord, don't you care that my sister has left me
to do the work by myself?
Tell her to help me!'

'Martha, Martha,' the Lord answered,
'You are worried and upset about many things,
but few things are needed

— or indeed only one.
Mary has chosen what is better,
and it will not be taken away from her."

Martha and Mary lived in Bethany, just over the other side of the Mount of Olives, a short walk from Jerusalem. I imagine Martha would have been excited to receive Jesus into her family home. How wonderful to have the Saviour come.

I imagine what I would do if Jesus came to my house. I am sure I would be up early cleaning the house within an inch of its life, sparkling bathrooms, fresh sheets on the bed in case the disciples decided to stay, and a magnificent meal. My speciality is a beautiful slow-cooked lamb roast with multiple sides, fresh bread from Baker's Delight, not from the supermarket, cheese platters, and some chocolate-covered profiteroles for dessert. I imagine it would be like when you are hosting Christmas, but on a grander scale. Luckily enough, I would have a family I could count on, knowing my sister would help.

Jesus arrives early! The house is not as clean as I would like; the disciples drop their filthy sandals at the door, and I am still in my trackies. I feel a little taken aback, but I am a great host and will quickly get changed and get back on track. The roast is already cooking; I just need to organise the sides. My sister will help with this. As I begin in the kitchen, I hear muffled noises from the lounge room and Jesus speaking, but I don't know what He is saying. Occasionally, I can listen to the people and disciples laugh or ask questions, but honestly, I can't get a gist of what is happening. I go into the back to find my sister because if we do not get the veggies on soon, there will be no sides for lunch, which would be a disaster.

As I walk past the room where Jesus is teaching, I notice my sister sitting at Jesus' feet, listening to every word He says. I am furious; how could she be so inconsiderate? I walk past the doorway once, twice, finally three times - trying to get her attention. Just to make matters a little worse, I am also giving her the evil eye with a quick jolt of my head, like get yourself out here, but she looks at me and then totally ignores me.

By this time, I have been awake for hours. I am tired and feel abused by the whole situation. Let's be honest: I am not a gracious host anymore. I am annoyed and feeling quite taken advantage of. Not only that, but I have decided it is only fitting that I interrupt Jesus and His teachings to bring to His attention the abuse happening back here in the privacy of my kitchen.

"Excuse me, Jesus, (with just a little tone), could I just grab Mary? We have a few things in the kitchen to attend to."

After looking down and smiling at my sister, He looks me straight in the eye and says, "Beautiful girl, you are worried and upset about many things, but few things are needed—or, indeed, only one. Your sister has chosen that which is better, and it will not be taken away from her."

I was humiliated. Why was Jesus speaking to me like this? After all, could He not see I was hurt? I was now bitter, helping begrudgingly, and regretting opening my home for any of this at all. Surely, He could see I was in the right, and she was in the wrong!

When I started the ladies' group, my loving sister was my encouragement. Initially, the group started because we had both left our old congregation. I had spoken before about some of the complexities regarding this move. We missed them; they were like our extended family. We missed their fellowship and wanted to recreate this in a fresh, new way. It was hard to meet people in such a big church, and we were fabulous, but we were the brand-new girls on the block.

We decided to step out in courage and invite some of these girls on Sunday to a coffee shop the following Wednesday. It was a little scary, but as we began to invite these girls, do you know what happened? We met a lot of beautiful women who were also lonely and wanted to connect.

We both arrived at the coffee shop early, nervous and a little giggly. We kept saying that if no one came, we would at least have each other and still have a good night. But right on the dot of 7:00 pm, the girls started flooding in – it was truly wonderful.

Eventually, we did not just want it to be a night of connection but an opportunity to pray for women and discuss the Word, so as my sister lived in the country, we decided to change the location to my house.

I can remember that first night before everyone came, I was the perfect amount of excited and nervous. I found myself scrubbing the skirting boards with a toothbrush an hour before everyone was due to arrive! Not only that, but I didn't realise my house was so dusty. My sister called amid this craziness, not like Mary, and asked if she could help me in any way. I explained that I was cleaning my skirting boards with a toothbrush, and she laughed. She said, "Just rest, it is going to be ok. We have invited the girls and created the space – God's going to do the rest".

She immediately stopped me in my tracks; I dropped the toothbrush and placed it back in the cupboard. It did not matter if my house was perfect. All I needed was God – He was the focus, not me or the cleanliness of my home. She freed me just to be me. I was acceptable and did not need to be perfect, as this was all about my amazing Saviour.

How often do we find ourselves hyper-fixated on something completely irrelevant because we do not want to face the task or issue at hand? We are trying any way we can to escape anxious thoughts or moments, using control or, in my case, cleaning to distract or make our worries disappear. Sometimes, we need an amazing sister – to step in and point us back to Jesus. Let's be that sister to each other.

Now, going back to Martha and Mary. I love that Jesus was wise enough when Martha asked that important and fateful question, that he didn't just answer her at face value but travelled through time to consider every woman who puts their family first, who sacrifices their all. Instead of validating our role in the kitchen or as the cleaner or carer, He welcomed us to the lounge room and invited us to join

His discussion. He did not leave us stuck but reminded us how important we are in His ministry. He set us free from a life where our value was only found in what we could do for God or others.

He truly saw our frustration at being minimised and marginalised in society. He set examples that every person was valuable to God and that we all belong at the table. He set a precedent that we are all important and that He wants to connect with each of us personally:

Galatians 3 v 28 NIV

"There is neither Jew nor Gentile,
there is neither slave nor free,
there is no male and female;
for you are all one in Christ Jesus."

So today, He gently calls all of us again into the lounge room to sit and hear the good news. As I sit in my little worn velvet armchair,

He whispers,

"Come, precious daughter,
come and spend time with me.

Come read my love letter from home
and remember who you are."

Let us **never** be so busy in the kitchen, or any other place, that we miss spending time with our amazing Jesus again.

CHAPTER TWELVE

Be Still

Psalms 46 v 10 NIV

"BE STILL and **KNOW** that I am God".

This is one of the most important of God's revelations. We all face moments when our lives seem to be spinning out of control, our hearts begin to race, fear or anger begins to overwhelm us, and we try to take control.

There is nothing quite like the world falling apart around us (both literally and figuratively) to highlight our false beliefs about control. Sure, I know I cannot control everything, but as a daughter, a wife, a mother and a grandmother, it definitely feels like my responsibility to do so.

Here is the amazing thing, shifting my focus from trying to control everything and everyone around me to surrendering control to God has given me the ability to create a life of peace.

The Hebrew word for "still," used in the Psalms (Raphah), means to sink, relax, and let go. How beautiful. Often, this is the last thing we want to do when the world is spinning, and we feel like we have limited control over our lives or situations.

In Queensland, Australia, we have multiple theme parks. One of my favourite memories is going to Wet and Wild with my family back in the 1990s. There was a particular ride called Calypso Beach. After a crazy day of waterslides and swimming, you can sit back and relax in a soft inner tube as you float around a lazy river, drifting through subtropical gardens - it is so beautiful. The ride has a gentle current, so as you rest in your tube, it takes you through a journey of different landscapes and seasons, just like life. It is very relaxing, but if you stepped out of the tube and decided you were going to swim against the current, it would not take long before you would become completely exhausted by the effort.

In life, I often think about being still in this context, a life of surrender. Trusting God - engaging a calm and peaceful posture of strength, as **God** directs our paths and fights our battles.

Of course, it is really easy to trust God when He is running your life the way you desire, but how do you cope in a time of sorrow, pain or chaos? Can we still fully engage in this process? Genuinely letting go and letting God take control of our lives becomes much more difficult.

When darkness envelops us, we often wrestle with giving control to the one with the power to bring us through it. He is the God who knows our first breath to our last and every breath in between. Being still and knowing He is God means moving to a new level of trust, a level that will challenge our faith in remarkable ways.

If we honestly believe that God is good and that His character is love, why would we not be giving control to Him all the time? Why wouldn't we always run towards Him for safety and help?

In the most challenging times of my life, I repeat to myself "Beautiful girl – your steps are ordered by the Lord, remember this." Immediately, it reminds me of God's heart for my life. It helps me not to buy into the fallacy that I control anything. This means being still and watching God as He does His work, fully engaged in the process as we trust and rest in Him.

Remember - Proverbs 3 v 5–6 NKJV

"Trust in the LORD with all your heart;
and lean *not* to your own understanding.
In all your ways acknowledge him, and
He will direct your paths."

In the contemporary English version, it says-

**"Always let Him lead you,
and He will clear the road for you to follow."**

Or, in the Holman Christian version -

**"Think about Him in all your ways,
and He will guide you on the right paths."**

Surrendering is not the same as giving up — not when God is involved. Submitting to God means humbly placing ourselves at His feet and giving up our pride and desire for control. Under the care of God's mighty hand, we release the need to know the answers to all of the big questions.

The Whens?
The Whys?
The Hows?

We need to stop at the crossroads because we have a choice. Do we want to be in control, with no insights into the future, no ability to necessarily change people's hearts or minds, and no capacity to heal or bind together, or do we choose God?

In "Hinds Feet on High Places," author Hannah Hurnard fictionalises the process of finding faith and then entering a life as a follower of Jesus as the Good Shepherd.

The story is based on Habakkuk 3 v 19: "The Sovereign Lord is my strength; he makes my feet like the feet of a deer; he enables me to tread on the heights or high places."

In this story, the main character, Much Afraid, is an orphan girl who wants to be healed and to escape her family and living situation. She meets the Good Shepherd, who offers to take her to the borderland of His Father's Kingdom, the Realm of Love.

He promises that although the journey will be difficult, He will go with her and give her hind feet, just like the scripture speaks of above. The invitation for Much Afraid was to follow and surrender completely to the ways of the Good Shepherd, just like the path of faith in our lives is a repeated invitation to surrender to God's will.

As she reaches the Father's Kingdom, the Realm of Love, she finds her heart is transformed, and her capacity to love changes from a longing to be loved by others to finding all her love in the Shepherd. She finally feels loved, significant, accepted, assured and secure in His love. This revelation helps her to recognise her authentic self, to sit in a place of wholeness and rest, and to find her true heart's desire.

This story is profound and a great representation of Jesus' love for us and our journey through life to return to the Heavenly Father.

Proverbs 23 NKJV, we read,

"The Lord is my shepherd;
I shall not want.

He makes me to lie down in green pastures;
He leads me beside the still waters.

He restores my soul;
He leads me in the paths of righteousness
For His name's sake.

> Yea, though I walk through the valley
> of the shadow of death,
> I will fear no evil;
>
> For You are with me;
> Your rod and Your staff,
> they comfort me.
>
> You prepare a table before me
> in the presence of my enemies;
>
> You anoint my head with oil;
> My cup runs over.
>
> Surely goodness and mercy shall follow me
> All the days of my life;
> And I will dwell in the house of the Lord
> Forever."

One afternoon, while I was busy working, a dear friend sent me this text.

> "How are you?
> I had a dream last night, and
> I would like to share it with you.
>
> I saw you sitting in your living room
> reading from Habakkuk, chapter three.
>
> I was sitting in front of you, and you shared
> with me this scripture, lifting your hands.
>
> You said to me, **Look** and I was amazed."

At the time, I was secretly going through a momentous trial so significant that it could break my family emotionally, physically, and financially. Our beautiful family was facing the perfect storm.

Now, knowing this godly woman, I was determined to wait until I returned home to read my old Bible, even though I had access to Google at work. I knew this was a message from God. It was precious, and I needed to give it reverence and weight for my life. As soon as I arrived home, I ran upstairs to the old velvet chair and grabbed my old KJV Bible, and this is what I read –

Habakkuk 3 v 17 NJKV

"Though the fig tree may not blossom,
Nor fruit be on the vines;

Though the labour of the olive may fail,
And the fields yield no food;

Though the flock may be cut off
from the fold,

And there be no herd in the stalls.

**Yet I will rejoice in the Lord,
I will joy in the God of my salvation.
The Lord God is my strength;**

> He will make my feet like the feet of a deer,
> He enables me to tread
> on the heights or high places."

At that moment, when everything was spinning out of control, and our future looked completely changed, I was unsure if we would be able to survive the horrific disaster that was unfolding. God was there. He reminded me of my faith. **He reminded me of the joy of my salvation, and He reminded me He was my strength.**

What a blessing! I immediately began to cry. Here was God again, right by my side, saying,

> "Precious girl, I am with you.
>
> Do not fear; I hear you."

God promises in Isaiah 61 1-3, 7

> "The Spirit of the Sovereign Lord is upon me,
>
> for the Lord has anointed me
> to bring good news to the poor.
>
> He has sent me to comfort the broken-hearted,
>
> and to proclaim that captives will be released
> and prisoners will be freed.
>
> To all who mourn in Israel, he will give a

crown of beauty for ashes,

oil of joy instead of mourning,

**and spirit of praise instead
of a garment of heaviness.**

In their righteousness,
they will be like great oaks that the Lord
has planted for his own glory.

Instead of shame and dishonour,
you will enjoy a double share of honour.

You will possess a double portion
of prosperity in your land,
and everlasting joy will be yours."

This scripture is powerful. I love these words because it describes who we are and who God is. If you are reading this book and travelling through the battle of your life, I want to encourage you.

Be STILL and KNOW God.

He is your strength; lean on Him. He will bring you joy again - in Jesus' name – Amen.

CHAPTER THIRTEEN

Singing in the Wilderness

What does the wilderness mean to you? For me, the wilderness is a place of hopelessness, darkness, insecurity and isolation—a feeling of being unloved and unaccepted. In the Oxford dictionary, "wilderness" means a neglected or abandoned and inhospitable environment.

If you have followed Jesus for any length of time, you will know what the wilderness is like, and if you have not yet hit a wilderness patch, you will. It is part of life here on earth, and rather than wishing it away, I would like you to learn how to "wander well" within it.

In Australia, but especially in the southern state where I am from, if you decide to travel by car, you often have to drive for hours and hours to reach some of the larger cities on the East Coast. There is a very long stretch of road every traveller loathes as you hit New South Wales called the Hay Plains. This vast expanse of flat land and saltbush is counted in the top three flattest places on earth and is voted by my family as one of the most boring places to travel through. It takes hours to get from one town to the next. On one of our family adventures to the East Coast, with kids asleep in the back seat of our station wagon, my husband and I made our way through this part of our Australian wilderness.

We noticed an unusual black cloud in the distance coming towards us. Initially, we thought it was a small thundercloud, but as it came closer, we saw it moved differently. It was a large swarm of locusts. As the day turned to night and the first locusts began hitting our car, we watched with intrigue as we travelled through a sea of insects. It was magnificent and terrifying as the swarm enveloped our vehicle. It was all-consuming. Every window was covered in these little creatures, yet they continued to move on. What I noticed most was how the atmosphere changed, being encompassed by their presence. It was overwhelming. There were thousands upon thousands of them. They blocked the daylight and made everything dark. Days later, we found them caught in every nook and cranny of our car. I now want to jump into the story of Gideon in Judges 6-8 in the NIV:

> "Because the power of Midianites
> was so oppressive,
> the Israelites prepared shelters for themselves
> in mountain clefts, caves and strongholds."

How often do we build and hide in caves of anxiety or pits of depression in times of trouble? When facing trials, our natural desire is to place hedges of protection around ourselves and everything we hold precious. This can quickly become a prison of isolation and a stronghold, just like the Israelites encountered.

> "Whenever the Israelites planted their crops,
> the Midianites, Amalekites and other
> eastern peoples invaded the country".
>
> They camped on the land
> and ruined the crops of Gaza
> and did not spare a living thing for Israel,
> neither sheep nor cattle nor donkeys.
>
> The Midianites came up with their livestock
> and their tents like **swarms of locusts**.
>
> It was impossible to count them or their camels;
> they invaded the land to ravage it."

The Israelites were overwhelmed, facing a sea of enemies described by the Bible as a **swarm of locusts** who turned their lives to darkness. They impacted and destroyed everything in their path, extinguishing the Israelites' hopes and dreams. This is where we meet Gideon.

> "The angel of the Lord came and sat down
> under the oak in Ophrah
> that belonged to Joash the Abiezrite,
> where his son Gideon was threshing wheat
> in a winepress to keep it from the Midianites."

> "When the angel of the Lord appeared
> to Gideon, he said,
>
> **The Lord is with you, mighty warrior."**

Now Gideon was hiding, threshing wheat in a hole in the ground because he was too scared to be out in the open air. Threshing wheat is loosening the edible part of grain from the straw and husks. This process is usually performed outside in the open air so the wind can blow away the chaff. When the angel of the Lord found Gideon, he was anything but a mighty warrior. He was traumatised by his current living situation and frightened even to step outside into the open air. He was hiding from the world, from his life and his family.

> "Pardon me, my lord, Gideon replied,
> But if the Lord is with us,
> why has all this happened to us?
>
> Where are all his wonders that our ancestors
> told us about when they said,
>
> Did not the Lord bring us up out of Egypt?'
>
> But now the Lord has abandoned us
> and given us into the hand of Midian."
>
> The Lord turned to him and said,
>
> **Go in the strength you have**
>
> and save Israel out of Midian's hand.

Am I not sending you?"

Pardon me, my Lord,
Gideon replied, But how can I save Israel?

My clan is the weakest in Manasseh,
and I am the least in my family.

The Lord answered,

I will be with you."

When we find ourselves in a prolonged time of walking in the wilderness, we can often begin with the "Whys."

Why has God abandoned me,
Why is He punishing me, and
Why does He not love me? - just like Gideon.

In this passage of scripture, we see how God tells Gideon to **"Go in the strength he has"**. He does not require him to have supernatural power or strength but asks him to go in the strength he already has. We know this is God's request to us even now: to take courage and go with the strength we have. God promises He will be with us and will not forsake us. He will do the rest.

I love how God continually bridges the gap between our abilities and the calling of His purpose. He stoops down to engage us, to love us, to speak over us, and to let us also hold a part of His victory.

God often chooses the weakest to do His bidding which I believe shows contrast and highlights His true strength.

In whatever area of weakness we find ourselves, don't rule yourself out of your God-given purpose or destiny. The Holy Spirit "Can stand in the gap" between our capacity and God's purpose.

Further down in the story, we find Gideon questioning again if he is indeed the man for the job and if he can trust God to perform this incredible miracle. Many Christians argue the concept regarding signs and wonders and whether God would only perform a miracle for the strong of faith. Here, we find Gideon frightened, lacking in faith, and testing God's commitment to his circumstances.

"Gideon said to God,

If you will save Israel by my hand
as you have promised

— look, I will place a wool fleece
on the threshing floor.

If there is dew only on the fleece
and all the ground is dry,

then I will know that you will save Israel
by my hand, as you said.

And that is what happened.

Gideon rose early the next day;
he squeezed the fleece and

wrung out the dew – a bowlful of water.

Then Gideon said to God,

Do not be angry with me.
Let me make just one more request.

Allow me one more test with the fleece,

but this time, make the fleece dry
and let the ground be covered with dew.

That night, God did so.

Only the fleece was dry;
all the ground was covered with dew."

How patient is God as Gideon gingerly steps towards his purpose? This is a man who is living in a cave, frightened to perform his daily tasks outside. It would be the equivalent of today's life of putting down the roller shutters, watching copious amounts of Netflix, ordering all his meals, shopping online and, of course, eating Cadbury chocolate. Hmmm, who does that sound like? Yet God carefully and lovingly shows that He is with Gideon. He doesn't get angry at Gideon's lack of faith or disqualify him from stepping into this significant role in history. He knows the trauma and pain he has endured. He is whispering to Gideon – you are God's BELOVED child.

After the miracle of the fleece, we again see God up the

ante. He reduces Gideon's army from thousands to three hundred by supernaturally helping him select the most battle-ready. Remember, Gideon was facing a mammoth task; you would think having more men would be an advantage. God wanted to make it clear to His people and the Midianites that He was fighting this battle (remember, the Midianites were like a plague of locusts in the land; their numbers were countless). It would take a miracle for 300 men to succeed against such a large enemy.

I want to encourage you today. If you feel overwhelmed by your circumstances or if you have a mammoth task or battle ahead, don't give up. This is where our Almighty God does his best work.

So, God sends Gideon's army down to the river to refresh themselves and drink from the water. As He does, he asks Gideon to observe them,

> "The Lord said to Gideon,
> With the three hundred men
> that lapped the water.
>
> I will save you and give the Midianites
> into your hands.
>
> Let all the others go home.
>
> So, Gideon sent the rest of the Israelites home
>
> but kept the three hundred, who took
> over the provisions and trumpets of the others.

Now, the camp of Midian
lay below him in the valley.

During that night, the Lord said to Gideon,

Get up, go down against the camp
because I am going to give it into your hands.

If you are afraid to attack, go down
to the camp with your servant Purah
and listen to what they are saying.

Afterwards, you will be encouraged
to attack the camp.

Gideon arrived in the enemy camp
just as a man was telling a friend his dream.

'I had a dream,' he was saying.

'A round loaf of barley bread came tumbling
into the Midianite camp.

It struck the tent with such force
that the tent overturned and collapsed.'

His friend responded,

'This can be nothing other than
the sword of Gideon, son of Joash, the Israelite.

God has given the Midianites and the

whole camp into his hands."

I love this part of the story because it shows while Gideon was terrified of the Midianites, they were already expecting defeat.

> "When Gideon heard the dream
> and its interpretation,
> he bowed down and worshipped.
>
> He returned to the camp of Israel and called out,
> 'Get up!
>
> The Lord has given the Midianite camp
> into your hands.'
>
> Dividing the three hundred men
> into three companies,
> he placed trumpets and empty jars
> in the hands of all of them,
> with torches inside.
>
> 'Watch me,' he told them.
> 'Follow my lead.
>
> When I get to the edge of the camp,
> do exactly as I do.
>
> When I and all who are with me blow our trumpets,
> then from all around the camp
> blow yours and shout,
>
> 'For the Lord and Gideon."

So, with three hundred men, trumpets, torches and jars, the Lord caused the Midianites throughout the camp to turn on each other and, in all the chaos, eventually flee.

It is an utterly amazing passage of scripture where God uses the small, the insignificant and the weak to become mighty. This story is once again good news, especially if you feel unworthy or ill-prepared. God is asking you not to take yourself out of stepping into His destiny, but this can make you ideal for the job. God never needs perfect or strong people; He needs prayerful and willing ones. We see how God calls our future into our present, as He calls Gideon a mighty warrior while hiding in a cave. Ask God to describe your calling; let him speak specifically. Don't be surprised if you are shocked at what He reveals to you. Remember, God does not call the qualified; He qualifies the called. What is He calling you to?

Many years later, my husband and I cruised to New Zealand and travelled to the Bay of Islands. This beautiful destination has calm, sandy beaches, abundant marine life, and lush native forest, making it a true paradise.

While there, we decided to visit one of New Zealand's natural wonders. With our guide, we followed a wooden boardwalk through 200 metres of dark limestone cave. We were asked to hold our torches at our feet as we walked. It reminded me of this scripture:

Psalms 119 v 105 NIV

"Your word is a lamp for my feet
and a light for my path."

As we entered the cave, we could hear rushing water beneath us and found ourselves in complete darkness, apart from the little light at our feet.

Eventually, after trekking a fair distance, the guide asked us to turn off our lights. It was so dark I could wave my hand in front of my face and could not see it. It was like a hole, a shelter, a stronghold in the ground. The darkness was nearly suffocating. As our eyes adjusted, she asked us to look up, and there, to my joy and amazement, was a spectacular ceiling full of what looked like chandeliers of sparkling glow worms. It was one of the most beautiful and glorious things I had ever seen.

As we looked above, the guide began to sing an old psalm, her voice echoing throughout the cave chambers. I can only say the whole experience was stunning and incredibly moving. I could not help but marvel at our Creator and how God created beauty even in the darkest cave, in the darkest hole—just because He could.

Psalms 65

"He is the God who created the mountains,
the roaring seas, the meadows,
and the flocks that graze upon them.

He proclaims,
"The whole earth is filled
with awe at your wonders;
where morning dawns, where evening fades,
you call forth songs of joy."

I encourage you not to give up the next time you find

yourself walking through the wilderness. Remember, God sees you, even in those caves of anxiety or pits of depression. Don't let this moment become the prison or your stronghold. Remind yourself of Gideon and go with the strength you have; God will do the rest. You are not excluded, and you are not too broken. God loves you and wants you to touch the miracle, so step out in the daylight and be brave because,

>The Lord says, "**I will be with you.**"
>
>**Amen**

CHAPTER FOURTEEN

Living in Paradise

Many years ago, we went to see my beautiful sister and her family for Christmas. They were living in a small town outside of Hobart, Tasmania. It was a wonderful opportunity to bring all of our children together and enjoy the holiday season.

That night, we stayed at the Hotel Grand Chancellor but awoke to the tragic news of a large tsunami in the Indian Ocean. The Boxing Day tsunami was unfortunately believed to be the deadliest tsunami in history, killing hundreds of thousands of people across fourteen countries. People in the tsunami's path were taken by surprise and limited evacuations were conducted before its impact. Reports showed the sheer scale of the devastation, with entire communities wiped out by the force of the wave. It was chilling.

Earthquakes, tornados, hurricanes, tsunamis, typhoons,

cyclones, mudslides, and wildfires. Natural disasters can be frightening and devastating for all those impacted. Horrific pictures and videos of families who have lost their homes and belongings, or worse, have suffered injury, death, or missing loved ones fill us with dread and sadness.

This can be a time when we can question whether God is truly good. Where was God during all of this? Couldn't He have prevented this destruction? Doesn't He care? Can we trust God?

To understand God's heart for our lives, we need to go right back. The good news story in the Gospels does not just start at the Cross of Christ. Understanding the good news starts by understanding God's original design, dream, and purpose for our lives.

The Bible starts in Genesis, where God deliberately designs humanity to enjoy a personal relationship with Him. We see, as God spoke, He created. The power of His words brought creation to life. This is the reason why we should never doubt His promises. His spoken word is so powerful it has no choice but to bring and create life. In Genesis, we see when He designed humanity, He changed His technique. When God created humankind, He stooped down and created us from the dust of the earth. He didn't just speak us into being. He made us with His very hands.

In creation, we see the first kiss in history as God breathes into Adam the breath of life. The Bible says he became a "living soul" made in the image of God. This idea alone can transform the way you view your life and how you view others. You were created in the image of God, with dignity, honour and respect. You were created to think, feel and dream. You can love, cry, dance and sing. You are not an accident. You were made with a plan in mind with incredible beauty, dignity and purpose.

God's original design was that we would have a personal relationship with Him and walk in the cool afternoon breeze of a garden paradise. How wonderful! He intended that we would live in paradise, a thriving place, not a broken place. God created beauty, abundance and rest. He created boundaries to care for us and keep us safe. This natural order was a cycle of **LIVING, GIVING** and **LOVING**. We see this now all through creation in cycles of nature. We see this in photosynthesis, the process by which plants make oxygen in the air that we breathe. We also see this in the water cycle, which follows the movement of water around the earth from liquid water, solid ice and water vapour gas; nurturing every living thing.

In Genesis, we see how we were able to eat from every tree, including the Tree of Life; the only one considered forbidden was the Tree of Knowledge of Good and Evil.

We all know the story: Adam and Eve partook of this tree and invited sin, greed, sickness, and selfishness into our world. Unfortunately, many of us in society are still eating from this tree, and the impact of this has been devasting to humankind.

When we live from the Tree of Life – God provides all our

needs. He is the centre of everything, and we find rest.

When we eat from the Tree of Knowledge of Good and Evil, we place ourselves at the centre of our lives. We don't sit from a place of abundance but a place of fear—fear of not having enough, a place of selfishness and controlling others.

We lose trust in others and judge ourselves harshly, asking questions like, Am I good enough? Is this person well-intentioned, or can I truly trust them? We start to live from anxiety instead of rest. We want to control not only our lives but others as well. We become fearful or selfish, not sharing the abundant resources that were designed for all of humanity.

This is the broken world and society we live in. We see famine, pain, suffering, loss, and sickness. We sadly see a disrespect for the earth we live on and the people who dwell in it. It becomes more important to own resources, stockpile wealth, show success, and influence others rather than loving and valuing the people and the paradise God has given us.

We see consumerism—and its constant production of meaningless products—leading to the depletion of natural resources and affecting the natural order.

But God is always calling us back to a place of relationship with Him, a life of abundance, where we love Him and love others, eating once again from the Tree of Life.

Much of the pain and suffering we experience today can be attributed to the selfishness of others or our insatiable desire to feed our spiritual needs from things other than God.

The lack of resources in the community can often be due to the greed of others. I do wonder if everyone started loving God, and loving others, would we find ourselves living in paradise once again? As we have read before, Jesus says,

John 10 v 10 NKJV

"The thief does not come except to steal,
and to kill and to destroy.
**I have come that they may have life
and that they may have it more abundantly."**

In John 15, we see: **that Jesus is the True Vine**

"I am the true vine,
and My Father is the keeper of the vineyard.
He cuts off every branch in me that bears no fruit,
and every branch that does bear fruit,
He prunes to make it even more fruitful.

Remain in Me, and I will remain in you.
Just as no branch can bear fruit
by itself unless it remains in the vine,
neither can you bear fruit unless you remain in Me.

I am the vine, and you are the branches.
The one who remains in Me,

and I in him, will bear much fruit.
For apart from Me, you can do nothing."

Jesus wants us to connect back to the vine, Him—to the Tree of Life. He wants to be the lifeblood that runs through our veins; He wants to remind us of the Father, the Vine keeper who tenderly prunes us to make us strong and grow.

You will notice in this passage; that we only bear fruit; we don't produce it. It is not in our own strength but is due to the life force that runs through us as we stay connected to the vine, Jesus. We don't produce fruit; we just have the privilege to bear it. This is good news, as it means we don't have to run ourselves in circles to be good, to be acceptable or pleasing to God. We become acceptable, fully pleasing, and fully forgiven through a life abiding and connected to Jesus.

Our mission is not to live a life where we judge ourselves and others, eating from the Tree of Knowledge of Good and Evil, but to stay connected to Jesus, the Tree of Life, to love God and love others.

Remember - If we focus on sin – it will win.
We must always focus on Him.

2 Corinthians - 5:17 ESV

"Therefore, if anyone is in Christ,
he is a new creation.
The old has passed away;

behold, the new has come."

We have a choice. Do we open our hearts to Jesus, or do we continue to be a branch disconnected from the vine, slowly dying? God gives us the choice of whether we love him or not, whether we want to stay connected to Him or not, and finally, whether we want to trust Him or not. We get to choose wholeness through God, how we meet our spiritual needs and how we see the importance and destiny of our lives.

In Tasmania, we made our way to Bagdad, a camping complex, where we stayed for the New Year period with many other families, including my sister, her husband, and three children. While we were there, we met two couples who had recently travelled to Vanuatu on a mission trip. They told us of their amazing experiences, their testimonies, and the goodness of God, which captured our hearts.

They mentioned trekking through the rainforests of Efate when they came across an isolated village. While staying in Port Villa, they were hoping to meet with a fellow from the church they were attending. As they arrived, the community asked if they could pray for a man who had not walked for many years. My friend spoke of his worry: What would happen if God did not heal him? How would the local villagers perceive it? As they moved into the very humble dwelling in their village, in the back corner lay a man unwell on a makeshift bed. They talked to him for a while and asked if he would like some prayer. He had a significant standing in his community, being Chief of his village. They began to pray, both in English and in their Heavenly language, when all of a sudden, he started to wriggle and move his feet and within a short space of time, he motioned to stand. While this was going on, the whole community was outside his home waiting to see the outcome of the prayer. When this man stood, with the support of my friends, and walked out of his dwelling, the community were shocked with disbelief. (Actually, so was my friend who told the story.) There were tears, ululating, and celebrations. It was a miracle!!

As they described their experiences, we were hooked and booked a trip to attend with them in late May. It was an amazing opportunity for our whole family. We travelled to many extraordinary places on the back of old pickup trucks. We met people who lived so simply that it humbly made us realise how excessive our own country and western lives were.

I recall one particular day we trekked through a rainforest to a clearing to meet the original Chief and some of the friends from the previous trip. We saw all these children playing in the trees, holding little knives that they were using to cut the abundant fruit growing in the rainforest.

I watched as my children looked up and waved at them. Here were these little ones with such freedom and such a connection to nature and each other, yet at home, my children were often inside and barely allowed to play on the street.

Once we arrived at the village, we were greeted with homemade leis and an adorable older lady named Mary.

She was a grandmother who offered us a drink of red cordial, which she had specially purchased from the shop many kilometres away. Mary served this precious drink in any dish she could borrow or find. I was so honoured by her generosity.

It reminded me of the story of the widow with two mites in Luke 21 v 1-4. Jesus was teaching His disciples in the temple when:

> "He looked up and saw the rich people
> dropping offerings in the collection plate.
> Then he saw a poor widow put in two pennies.
>
> He said The plain truth is that this widow
> has given by far the largest offering today.
> All these others made offerings
> that they will never miss;
> she gave extravagantly what she couldn't afford,
> **she gave her all!**"

That day, we prayed and saw people healed, baptised people in the river, and sang acoustic islander versions of psalms and songs we knew from home. It was amazing to see the same God in all His glory in the middle of the South Pacific Ocean, stooping down and personally connecting to each one of us.

As we sat around fires in the evening and sang songs, we brought little gifts for the children. We watched with delight as they played with bouncy balls, and matchbox cars and enjoyed lolly pops as if they were priceless treasures. I remember walking back to the pick-up truck and finding one such lolly pop tangled in my hair. What a fun memento; I am sure some little one must have lost it in all the excitement.

Later in the evening, we would stumble into our resort after travelling many uncomfortable hours on the back of utes. Each night we would return to see people swimming and drinking by the pool or bar. All four of us would walk past them covered in mud and dirt from our trips, with homemade leis around our necks and smiles from ear to ear. We looked like we had just competed on an episode of Australian Survivor. We were a sight to see, so people asked about our experiences, and once again, we were able to share the goodness of God. It was voted as one of the best family trips ever.

One night, my daughter and I gathered with the women in the local community and discussed the differences between our two cultures. I explained how appreciative my family were of their hospitality and in awe of their lives and community. They spoke so humbly of their faith and ability to trust God in such a fresh way that it changed my perspective completely. They humbly spoke of only owning small and simple things. One woman said that it was much harder for us in Australia to have faith as we owned big things which provided big distractions that would block us from seeing the goodness of God. She was completely right.

Mary was a true leader and a great example of a godly woman. She would walk three hours to and from church every Sunday with her little grandson strapped to her back. The last day of our trip was the most difficult as it was time to say goodbye. When I told Mary we were leaving, she asked if we were coming back, but unfortunately, I had to explain it was our last day. I could see in her eyes she was sad, that we would not spend another day together. What she said next captured my heart, she exclaimed:

> "My beautiful friend,
> we will see each other in Paradise."

I was overwhelmed with joy when she sang, jumped, ululated, and waved to us as we boarded our flight back to Australia.

I look forward to that moment, when I see the beautiful Mary again.

CHAPTER FIFTEEN

Finding Peace

Now, my current experience is the hardest to share and document. It is the journey of my Father. He had moved from working in the Police force to joining the Fire Brigade. In 1989, he was awarded the national medal for his work with the SA Metropolitan Fire Service. A Commonwealth award that recognises people who risk their lives or safety to protect or assist the community. He was a leader in our previous church and was involved in pastoral care for the community.

During his late forties and early fifties, he had a significant shift in his thinking, became disillusioned with his faith, and found himself sitting in a place of indifference and depression, burnt out on religion.

Unfortunately, he had previously bought into the widespread acceptance of performance-based Christianity. If I do these things, God will love me, and I will be acceptable and perfect in His sight. Over the years, I have learnt this version of Christianity is incompatible with a joyful life. It robs us of the very promises of God - our peace and joy. Come to think of it, this story is proof that this approach is wrong, as it steals the very things God promises to give us - REST.

We reflect once more on this scripture:

Matt 11 v 28 – 10 MSG

"Are you tired? Worn out?
Burned out on religion?
Come to me.
Get away with me,
and you'll recover your life.

I'll show you how to take a real rest.

Walk with me and work with me
watch how I do it.

Learn the unforced rhythms of grace.

I won't lay anything heavy or ill-fitting on you.

Keep company with me, and you'll learn
to live **freely and lightly**."

In my Dad's case, I realised that the scriptures had become his rulebook rather than an invitation to a relationship with a loving God. This thinking caused a crushing weight of expectation that was too large or hard to meet. He couldn't see the **freely and lightly** but replaced the Good News with a view of not being good enough, abandoned, or rejected by God and His people.

There is clear evidence that this version of faith creates unhealthy and unsustainable thinking. The victorious Christian life morphs into what makes God love and accept me. If I am delivering at a high level, God is pleased and enjoys my company, but if I do not, God is not happy, and I better be fearful or do better quickly.

The disaster comes when we cannot deliver or keep up with this expected level of living. We can become critical, exhausted, and officially burn out.

Negative identity messages flourish, and we slowly drown in expectations of ourselves and others. This approach stops sustainable and long-term faith. Serving in church and community becomes a culture of perfectionism and competitiveness that controls us instead of releasing us to a life of true joy, true rest, and true freedom.

People caught up in this approach are faced with one of two choices. They can allow their pride to convince themselves that they are living up to this ideal, almost perfect life, which, of course, they are not. This way of thinking may lead to prideful, judgmental, and arrogant behaviour. Looking down on others, not loving them as Jesus asked. The perfect example of this is found in

Luke 18 v 10-14 NIV

Jesus speaks of the

The Parable of the Pharisee and the Tax Collector

"Two men went up to the temple to pray,
one a Pharisee and the other a tax collector.

The Pharisee stood by himself and prayed:
'God, I thank you that I am not like other people
robbers, evildoers, adulterers or
even like this tax collector.

I fast twice a week and give a tenth of all

But the tax collector stood at a distance.
He would not even look up to heaven,
but beat his breast and said,
'God, have mercy on me, a sinner.'

I tell you that this man,
rather than the other,
went home justified before God.

For all those who exalt themselves
will be humbled,

and those
who humble themselves
will be exalted."

The tax collector showed a humble example of repentance, but repentance is not just saying sorry. It is saying sorry with action to follow. A truly repentant heart will start an imperfect journey with the intention of living a life honouring God. They will not get it right every single time, but they will keep their eyes fixed on Jesus and continue to glorify His name. This pleases God, He wants us to live a life of honouring Him. He wants us to have a complete heart change – seeking our spiritual needs in Him.

Now, going back to the difficulties of performance-based religion, we read the disaster comes when we cannot deliver or keep up with a level of living as expected. We can become exhausted and officially burn out. The serious problem is it can be a vehicle for religious abuse, where we are trapped in a life of people-pleasing and feeling unable to safely say no to anyone who represents God. We can fall into wrongful thinking and reach a place of depression and despair, not believing we could ever be loved by God. We are still seeking our spiritual needs in others — it just happens to be other people of God! If we need someone's approval to sustain us, we are not free but caught in the grips of another. This is not God's plan for our lives. It is so important we don't get stuck here. God has shown us His heart for our lives and given us a way out of all this chaos, and His name is Jesus.

If you are in this space, I guarantee you will feel like you are missing something, and let me tell you, His name is Jesus Christ.

Ephesians 2 v 8–9 NIV

"For it is by grace you have been saved,
through faith,
and this is not from yourselves,
it is the gift of God.
Not by works, so that no one can boast."

God's Word says we are saved by grace through faith in Christ Jesus.

Grace means that God loves, forgives and saves us, not because of who we are or what we do, but because of the amazing work of Jesus.

The gospel message is good news because it sets us free from performance-based beliefs. We come to Jesus so grateful and loved that we can't help but fall into His arms. We are safe, secure, accepted, significant, loved, and assured, and finally, we find rest for our hearts and souls.

Our best efforts can **never** be good enough to earn our salvation. If there were any other way we could, then there would be absolutely no reason for Jesus to have died on the cross at all.

One way to understand the meaning of the death of Jesus is to imagine a courtroom scene in which we are on trial for our sins, and God is the judge. Our sins against God are capital crimes. According to divine law, our crimes deserve the death penalty.

Death, in a spiritual sense, means eternal separation from God in unending torment. By Jesus shedding His blood on the cross, He took the punishment we deserve and offered us **His righteousness.**

When we trust Christ for our salvation, we make a trade. By faith, we trade our sin and its accompanying death penalty for His righteousness and perfect life. Without Him, we would still suffer the death penalty for our sins, no matter how many good deeds we try to accomplish. This is a severe judgment.

In John 8, verses 1-11, we read about a woman who was caught in an intimate relationship with someone other than her husband.

To understand the context of this time, according to the Torah, both the man and woman were liable to be stoned to death by their community. This a serious situation, an actual life-and-death moment for this beautiful woman.

> "Jesus returned to the Mount of Olives,
> but early the next morning
> he was back again at the Temple.
>
> A crowd soon gathered,
> and he sat down and taught them.
>
> As he was speaking, the teachers of religious law
> and the Pharisees brought a woman
> who had been caught in the act of adultery.

They put her in front of the crowd.

'Teacher,' they said to Jesus,
'This woman was caught in the act of adultery.
The law of Moses says to stone her.

What do you say?'

They were trying to trap him
into saying something
they could use against him,
but Jesus **stooped down**
and wrote in the dust with his finger.

They kept demanding an answer,
so he stood up again and said,

**'All right, but let the one who has never sinned
throw the first stone!'**

Then he stooped down again and wrote in the dust.

When the accusers heard this,
they slipped away one by one,
beginning with the oldest,
until only Jesus was left in the middle
of the crowd with the woman.

Then Jesus stood up again
and said to the woman,

'Where are your accusers?
Didn't even one of them condemn you?'

'No, Lord,' she said.

And Jesus said,
'Neither do I - go and sin no more."

I love how, once again, we see Jesus profoundly change the thoughts of everyone in the room. He did not condemn in shame and guilt but loved this woman unconditionally, reminding her she was made for dignity and respect. We see His patience and kindness, just like the Heavenly Father.

Now, back to my Dad, during his life, Dad diligently served God and his community but became disillusioned with the level of control, expectations, and eventual heaviness he thought a life of faith held.

He burnt out from a life of trying to please God and others. He became frustrated with the Heavenly Father and His people and turned to a life focused naturally on fulfilling his spiritual needs.

Simultaneously, as a firefighter, he was called to a particularly hazardous fire at the Port Stanvac Oil Refinery. A record of this event reads like this:

Green Left, 1992, Issue 53 News. Adelaide, April 29, 1992:

"Fears have been raised that a fire at the Port Stanvac oil refinery in southern Adelaide on April 10 may have emitted toxic gases, polluting surrounding suburbs and residential areas. The Onkaparinga City Council, which covers the area, has called for a report from Mobil, the refinery owners, to include the risks to the community.

Council spokesperson said, 'We're seeking information on whether there were any toxic emissions due to the fire. We need to be aware of all the factors. It was a big ball of smoke, and we knew there were oil droplets in it. There is the potential for some pretty dangerous activity, and we need some answers to better understand. The fire, caused by equipment failure, sent a massive cloud of black smoke and fireballs into the air, visible up to 50km away".

Unfortunately, my Dad and many other brave firefighters were exposed to dangerous chemicals, including PFAS, which is now linked to thyroid disease, auto-immune disease, elevated levels of cholesterol, and testicular and kidney cancer.

Over many years, several of Dad's co-workers died prematurely due to cancer and respiratory-related deaths. It was not until after 9/11 in 2001, when the first responders of the terror attack simultaneously started suffering from similar respiratory and cancer-related diseases, that the world began to take notice and recognise the risk of early death due to exposure to harmful and toxic substances.

Our Father spoke of horrific circumstances that day and how the men bravely fought the fire towering many, many metres into the air. After the exposure, the firefighters noticed they were urinating a fluorescent-coloured discharge. They realised they had been saturated with toxic chemicals which could be harmful to their health.

More than a decade later, Dad received a diagnosis of non-Hodgins's lymphoma, later followed by kidney cancer, prostate cancer, and cancer of the lungs, brain, hip, eye and bones. Just recently, we received the devasting news that he was in stage 4 of his cancer journey and did not have long to live.

As a family, we decided to move Mum and Dad from their farm closer to the family so we could support them in his care. As always, God's hand was on the move, and after searching for a few months, a house came up near my home. It was perfect, and they soon moved in. I immediately took all my long service leave to spend time with them. Dad seemed joyful and at rest, and he spoke of this time being the happiest of his life.

We spent many days reading and discussing the Bible and its teachings; he even had some suggestions for the ladies' groups I was running. However, over the years, I have observed a barrier between Dad and his understanding of God's love, so I wanted to encourage him as he faces eternity. I remember discussing "God is Love" with him and the scripture in Corinthians, where we substitute the word 'Love' for 'God':

'Love' is patient, so 'God' is patient.

We discussed this verse at length; I remember Dad's reaction when we reached the part where **Love (God) does not traffic in shame or guilt and does not keep a record of wrongdoings.** He looked up immediately and said,

"Flick, does it really say that?"

I looked at him bewildered. Here was a man who had a long relationship with God but had struggled for many years to remember His goodness and faithfulness.

My memory goes back to when I was a small child when I saw him strong and faithful. I would find him preparing for another message, following up and supporting congregation members, or praying in his bedroom. Yet I wondered if this dedication had come from a sincere desire to please God but also from a place of proving to God he was worthy. We all know this is a difficult way to live.

Another day, I went to visit him, and he told me he had a nightmare. I asked him to describe the details. He mentioned he had died and gone to Heaven – but when he got there, God said, "There is one person who does not deserve to be here," and in his dream, he knew it was him.

I was shocked. How could he be thinking this so close to the end of his life? What was troubling his heart? I knew he had beliefs that were distorting God's character, but would we have time to identify them?

I continued to visit and chat over the months, and we had such a memorable time discussing the Word and enjoying each other's company.

I was determined to savour every moment with my Father before his passing, hoping he would **find peace**.

CHAPTER SIXTEEN

Set Free

It was mid-October, and I was going about my regular schedule getting ready for work when I noticed my parents' bins were not out on collection day. I ran over with my Husband to pull them onto the road when, surprisingly, a police car pulled up in their driveway—blocking our exit.

My Husband and I greeted the police officers. They mentioned that a stolen car had been left on the road behind this house and asked us who owned the property. When they asked if they could access the backyard, I mentioned that it was my parents' home.

My Husband took them round the back and chatted as he opened the gate. One of the police officers went to the back fence, where he produced what we were led to believe was a stolen black bumbag. He asked if we knew whether it was my parents' personal property.

By this time, my Mum had reached the back sliding door and was talking to the police officers herself. They asked again if our Father owned a bumbag. I said we were not really bumbag people and that they were welcome to take it.

Now I just want to take a moment and acknowledge all those gorgeous girls who occasionally rock a bumbag; my apologies. You go, girl; I just can't personally carry it off.

Now, he asked again if I could check with my Father before they left. I explained he was sick and asleep, as he struggled in the morning due to his cancer treatment, but I would go ask him and confirm verbally. The Police officers were adamant he needed to come to the back door and verify the stolen bag was not his.

Eventually, Dad came to the back sliding door, and at that very moment, a storm of concealed police officers rushed from around the front, past my Husband, Mum, and myself. They were yelling and screaming at my Dad – "GET DOWN!", cuffed and arrested him.

My Mum was in shock, crying. I remember saying, "Is this a joke? He used to be a police officer; he is very sick; please be gentle." I remember trying to advocate for him when two police officers pulled me to one side and said you need to stop – your Father is a bad man, and we have been looking for him for an exceptionally long time.

I was in shock; what did this mean? Surely, they had the wrong guy; this could not be our Dad. Eventually, he was taken in the patrol car, and we were left in complete devastation as police dogs and endless police officers searched the family home.

As we were led through the kitchen, I saw one of the officers searching our Dad's King James Bible—page by page. I immediately remembered him holding it while preaching to the congregation. I could not grasp what was happening. I looked at my Husband for comfort; we were both in shock; this all seemed so surreal.

After an hour or so, a detective finally confronted us, explaining why they were there. They had uncovered DNA evidence to suggest that our Dad had committed multiple bank robberies between 2004 and 2014. We were shocked and in disbelief; these crimes were committed up to 20 years ago.

Our dying Father was being placed in a holding cell waiting for his first court appearance, facing a list of charges, including multiple armed bank robberies. It was impossible to process. I asked the detective how long he could be in prison and if there was any chance he would be released on bail. Time was precious, he didn't have long to live. She mentioned that due to the seriousness of the crimes, there would be little hope of this. If he were found guilty, the penalty could be up to 20 years for each crime. We were utterly devastated.

As the mountains of evidence were gathered, we sadly began to lose hope that he was truly innocent. I remember standing at the end of the driveway the moment they found the semi-automatic rifle allegedly used in the robberies. I watched as the police officers and detectives cheered with glee in celebration. This was devasting for our family.

During the next six hours, police officers and detectives turned over every piece of furniture, paper, computer hardware, phones and objects in my parent's home and shed.

We were officially in a nightmare. I tried to reconcile the man I knew with the man they described. I remember holding my Husband's hand tightly as they discussed every detail of the allegations.

I looked across the room at my Sister and Mum, trying to focus on the moment. I struggled to believe what they were saying and what we were experiencing. They must be wrong. This is not the man we know.

I remember crying out to God, how could this be true? How could our Father have lied to us for so many years? This was all made much more complex with his cancer diagnosis.

I could not help but draw my memories back to the violence at the beach, my experience of my own significant and terrifying trauma. My heart broke for the bank tellers and bystanders who had been journeying through the violence of these events for the past 20 years.

We faced an enormous test of faith and a massive challenge in navigating the legal system. We coordinated prison visits and lawyers' appointments, had media camped on our street and lawn, drones above our homes, and photographers with telescopic cameras at our back fence. This was a big story in our hometown, as these crimes impacted many people. We were on every News channel, in the papers, on social media, and on messaging platforms.

The intensity of having your privacy shattered, press blocking your street and asking neighbours about your family. It was a nightmare and public shaming in all its glory.

I remember a journalist standing in my driveway with her camera pointing at my Mum's home, ready for the 4 pm News report crossover. It had been days of what felt like relentless bullying, and media camped out the front of our homes. I looked through my roller shutters. It was impossible to help my innocent Mum, who was trapped in her house only two doors down.

I had had enough. I knew that if I went out in the front yard and tried to ask them to stop, this would only antagonise and aggravate the situation further, and my face would be plastered all over the News. I felt powerless.

I stood in my home, asking the Lord for a strategy to make them go away when suddenly, I grabbed my portable speaker and opened the window just enough to place it on the ledge of my upstairs room. I googled worst music playlist ever and turned the volume to full. Well, I can only say the loudest, most awful music the reporters and I had ever heard came booming out of my window. To understand this fully, we live in a cul-de-sac on a hill, which is like a mini amphitheatre. The sound was deafening. The journalist, who was about to cross over to her team in the studio, turned and looked at my house. My heart began to beat fast as a woman in a very tight red dress with immaculate plastered hair and high heels ran across my front lawn, banging on the door. She was trying to stop the music from drowning out her voice. The team could not make the live crossover and missed their strict timeframe. For one beautiful moment, the story went quiet, and we had some peace. By the end of the day, the numerous vans and cars that had lined our street packed up their camera equipment and left! It was a small win in a time of complete craziness.

We were all dealing with betrayal and broken trust from our Father. I will never be able to fully describe the intensity of the next few months, apart from labelling it a constant cycle of the most traumatic emotions. There was anger, grief, loss, betrayal and sadness in all its many versions and within moments of each other.

There was intense public shaming and constant News articles as the story progressed. Our hearts were broken. But we knew nothing could compare to the victim's fear as they journeyed through that fateful day of the robberies, which changed their lives forever.

We found ways to cope by labelling our emotions before we spoke. This allowed us to communicate effectively and safely with each other. We soon realised that not everyone was processing or experiencing the same feelings at the same time. Announcing our emotions before speaking allowed us to express ourselves without triggering other family members in the room.

This one action provided a safe space to share our experiences and thoughts without judgment. It gave us an opportunity to acknowledge and validate the emotions of another. We allowed each other to feel different about the same situation and tried not to judge. It already felt like a whole community was weighing in on this situation; we needed to be kind and provide a safe place for each of us to sit. We needed to build tolerance and resilience to manage this time, so we prayed to God.

How would we survive this, and how would we deal with the shame and guilt within our community, workplaces, and church families? How could we face anyone? How could we attend work? How could we attend church? I knew there would be a real temptation to fall into a hole of isolation and a pit of depression, which I knew could become a stronghold of my life. This situation could easily become life-defining. I knew I could choose once again to pack up shop, put the roller shutters down, stay in my pj's, watch an excessive amount of Netflix (definitely not the News), and, of course, eat copious amounts of chocolate, just like I wanted to do all those years ago when I was attacked at the beach.

I promised myself that I would not hide or try to distract my mind. I would return to my place in the community within a week or two. I knew the temptation would be to push me into a stronghold or shelter of distraction, a place of isolation, but I needed my church family, encouragement, and God's biblical teaching. I knew that if I didn't connect to my spiritual family, the shame may become overwhelming and drown me.

I needed to hop onto the mat and let some of my beautiful friends carry me to the feet of Jesus.

In the story of Mark 2 v 3-11, we meet four friends who helped their paralysed friend to the feet of Jesus.

> "Some men came carrying
> a paralysed man on a mat
> and tried to take him into the house
> to lay him before Jesus.
>
> When they could not find a way to do this
> because of the crowd,
> they went up on the roof
> and lowered him on his mat
> through the tiles into the middle of the crowd,
> right in front of Jesus.
>
> When Jesus saw their faith, he said,
> Friend, your sins are forgiven.
>
> The Pharisees and the teachers of the law
> began thinking to themselves,
> Who is this fellow who speaks blasphemy?
> Who can forgive sins but God alone?
>
> Jesus knew what they were thinking and asked,
> Why are you thinking these things in your hearts?
> Which is easier:
> to say,

'Your sins are forgiven,'
or to say,
'Get up and walk?'

But I want you to know
that the Son of Man has authority
on earth to forgive sins.
So, he said to the paralysed man,
I tell you, get up,
take your mat and go home.

Immediately he stood up in front of them,
took what he had been lying on
and went home praising God."

I have always been a person who loves to support others and offer encouragement and prayer, but the level of attack paralysed me.

I needed friends to help me. In the first week, when I once again attended church, many of my friends who were aware of the situation were there to greet us. A gentleman approached my husband just before the first service he mentioned, "Did you hear the news about the man they caught for all those bank robberies? He had previously attended the church down the road." He knew we had attended that church, too, and asked if we knew him. Thankfully, my husband took complete control of the conversation as I stood there like a stunned mullet. As I sat in my seat before the service, my husband looked at me, his eyes glistening, and he made me smile. It was absurd; this man did not know me, did not know my Father, and didn't know I was his daughter. I faced my fear and found it was not that hard. How could this be our life now? This man was interested in the latest hot story or gossip and was sharing the local news. It was all just so ridiculous.

As we walked through the many court appearances, we were again surrounded by the media. Not a day went by when one of us did not cry; it was so painful and hurtful. How would we recover?

There were also financial implications for our beautiful and innocent Mum and possibly the extended family, as the Department of Public Prosecutions promised to take her home and all her finances in retribution for the funds stolen so many years ago. It was exhausting; just when we processed one part of this trauma, another terrible and more devasting part would begin to play out. There was a significant worry that they may turn to the extended family to recover Dad's debt, and I remember thinking they might take everything we owned, too.

None of us knew about these crimes, but who would believe us? I had tried to live an honest and generous life, to help and love others, and to honour God. I remember praying, "All I have is my reputation and testimony. You know the truth; you know my values. Please let this pass; please help to set us free from any allegations."

As I cried in bed, I called out to God when this beautiful wave of peace came across me as my God comforted me.

The Word that came to me was:

" Precious girl,
they can take everything,
but they can't touch
the **One** that matters to you;

**they can never take the Comforter,
the Holy Spirit, your Heavenly language
and my strong connection to you.**"

This was a beautiful pearl of wisdom, a valuable and essential gift during this time in my life. At that moment, I knew everything was going to be okay.

The most challenging part of this process was the complexity of grappling with how this could be the man we knew. He was imperfect, but he was our Dad, a Husband, a Grandfather, and our GG.

I remember spending many days and nights praying for healing for the victims, protection for Mum, healing for her pain, for my broken heart and finally, forgiveness for Dad. Once again, I reflected on two of my favourite scriptures.

Psalms 34 v 18 NIV

"The Lord is closest to the broken-hearted,
he rescues those whose spirits are crushed."

Zephaniah 3 v 17 NIV

"He will take great delight in you,
He will quiet you with His love,

He will rejoice over you with singing."

I saw the goodness and mercy of friends, who dropped over meals and came to remind us we were strong and could get through this with God's blessing.

I remember talking to a dear friend when I asked, "How could I possibly continue to point people to Jesus?" My reputation felt in tatters. I felt a massive weight of shame that if I pointed to Jesus, I might somehow make Jesus less wonderful. My imperfect life and family situation would somehow impact God's reputation. I am a Christian, and my life is falling apart. She looked at me with kind eyes and said, "You need to rebuke that – that is the enemy speaking". She shocked me, but she was right. Jesus is not scared of our sins or our mess. He uses our weaknesses to create contrast, to be a testimony for His glory, and to turn our mess into a message. I found solace in my dearest friends as they prayed and supported me and as I continued to trust and call out to my God.

After a few weeks, we managed to apply to have Dad released on strict home detention, which was the first miracle of many. He was dropping weight so quickly due to his poor health. We did not know if he would survive his first months in prison or even make the trial.

We still needed to face a substantial emotional battle, not just for our family but for the healing of the victims and their families. The hundreds of lies, the betrayal of trust, the violence and trauma, how could we ever recover as a family? I knew this was an enormous battle and that it had the potential to break us if we did not pull together and trust God.

So now we face the final part of this journey – we have the choice to wait until the court trial scheduled for February 2025, in which case our Father will most likely die before it begins. Or he could choose to plead guilty, apologise to the beautiful victims and their families, and pay back every dollar of the stolen funds. We knew it could not fix the trauma and pain suffered but it could possibly start the journey of healing required for everyone involved. This means he returns to prison, an opportunity at least for some closure, maybe some eventual healing for the victims and their families.

As Dad faces his death with palliative cancer, it would be so easy to say, "Stay at home in the comfort of your favourite armchair, Dad", and not acknowledge to the community your mistakes. But we know God has called our family to more.

I remembered the dream Dad had explained about his thoughts on his worthiness of going to heaven. Could this moment be orchestrated by God? Could my precious God not allow my Dad to pass without setting things right?

Could He love him this much? What were the chances of him being caught 20 years later, months from passing away? It would be obvious that God would want to heal the pain and trauma of every person and family involved in these crimes, but could He also be moving to help in the life of my Dad? Would God be so generous?

I remember we discussed all the options and kept returning to the story of Jacob and Esau. Was Dad willing to swap his birthright for a pot of stew? He could easily stay quiet in the comfort of his home, die while on home detention, probably before he goes to trial, or he could claim his birthright, ask for forgiveness and make it right in front of God and his community. It was a huge ask; prison is truly the last place anyone wants to place someone you love dying of cancer.

Our Dad's actions were devastatingly wrong, and as he faces eternity, I wonder if God is saying – I love you, and I want you to make it right for the victims but also to set you free from shame and guilt.

So, as I sit here writing these final pages, my Father is sleeping nearby. He is shortly going to stand in front of all the people he hurt. He will sincerely apologise to them and the community and return to prison. It will be challenging, but I know it is God's plan.

I spoke to my Dad yesterday, as I helped him bring in the shopping. I told him I would always love him, not just to his, but to my very last breath as well. Even though he had committed these crimes many years ago, I forgave him. I was glad he was choosing the right path now, the only one of healing, redemption and forgiveness.

My last and most significant fear was the final moments of our Dad's life. Would he be alone? Would he be in pain? Would we be able to be with him? A beautiful friend of mine comforted me greatly by saying – you know Felicity, even if you can't be with your Dad when he passes, the Holy Spirit - the Comforter doesn't need permission or a day pass to join him in his cell. He will be with Him just like the scripture says.

Romans 5 v 5 NIV

"And hope does not put us to shame,
because God's love has been poured
into our hearts through the Holy Spirit
who has been given to us."

John 14 v 26 KJV

"But the Comforter,
which is the Holy Ghost,
whom the Father will send in my name,
he shall teach you all things,
and bring all things to your remembrance,
whatsoever I have said unto you."

1 John 1 v 9 NKJV

"If we confess our sins,
He is faithful and forgives us our sins
and to cleanse us from all unrighteousness."

Micah 7 v 19 describes NIV

"You (God) will again have compassion on us;
you will tread our sins underfoot and
hurl all our iniquities into the depths of the sea."

Ephesians 4 v 31-32 ESV

"Let all bitterness and wrath
and anger and clamour and slander
be put away from you,
with all malice,
and be kind to one another,
tender-hearted, forgiving one another,
as God in Christ forgave you."

And finally, my personal favourite

SET FREE

Romans 8 v 38 NLT

"And I am convinced
that nothing can ever
separate us from God's love.

Neither death nor life,
neither angels nor demons,
neither our fears for today

nor our worries about tomorrow
not even the powers of hell
can separate us from God's love.

No power in the sky
above or in the earth below
indeed, nothing in all creation
will ever be able to separate us
from the **Love of God**
that is revealed in Christ Jesus our Lord."

Amen.

I share this powerful testimony to show God's incredible love and forgiveness. If you are walking on a journey of forgiveness or currently sitting in a place of shame or guilt – I pray this last chapter will move powerfully in your life, that it will remind you that we all worship a God that has allowed us to be truly loved and truly forgiven.

Remember........

Who the Son sets free is **FREE INDEED**.

Acknowledgements

To my Heavenly Father, believing in you and what you say about me changes everything. I sincerely pray your words and love will continue to speak over future generations of my family. This book is a gift to ones I will never meet personally. I pray that our God will shine and impact every area of your life too. That His goodness will encourage you to love others courageously. That you will experience His love and know truly that you are **God's BELOVED child.**

In this book, I have purposefully referred to different translations of the Bible. I would encourage you not to be disheartened if you are struggling to read the Bible. The Word is God's love letter from home. As we read, our souls thirst to hear more from our Heavenly Father. I encourage you to go to your local Bible shop or online store and start reading different versions. I promise you there will be one that sings to you.

Let God show you the version that suits you. In my Bible study, I recommend and use the New King James, The Message, New Living Translation, New International Version, and the Passions translation.

I would like to acknowledge every reader who finds themselves in the pages of this book, and for the ladies who have attended my monthly Bible gatherings. Your wisdom, friendship, and guidance have been and continue to be a true inspiration.

I would like to make a special mention to the beautiful D Stevenson, whose guidance, dedication and mentorship has spoken over my spiritual life and many others profoundly.

Over the years, I have read many books, and much of the wisdom in this book has come from the Word, pivotal mentors and books on theology. Their wisdom has been sown deep into my heart, and for that, I am grateful. I have tried to acknowledge all, but over time, many of these thoughts have truly become my own.

So now I would like to have an Oprah moment, where I share some of **'my** favourite things' with the readers of this book. Each of these authors has profoundly touched my life and heart, so I suggest that they are must-reads for each of you.

M Stevenson, Pathway of Disciple by Edge Church International, 2022, SA, Australia. Also available through Equippers Church www.equippers.com.au.

ACKNOWLEDGEMENTS

Dr R Andrews, NewLife Worldwide Ministries' discipleship program, online material, Coffs Harbour, NSW, Australia.

Dr K Thompson, The Discipline of Suffering-Redeeming our stories of pain, 2023, Acorn Press, Sydney, NSW, Australia.

L TerKeurst, Forgiving what you can't forget, 2021, Thomas Nelson, US.

L TerKeurst, What happens when women say yes to God, 2018, Harvest House Publishers, Eugene, Oregon, US.

K Ruonala, Life with the Holy Spirit: Enjoying Intimacy with the Spirit and God, Charisma House, 2017, Florida, US.

K Ruonala, Double for your Trouble: Let God Turn your mess into a miracle, 2022, Charisma House, 2022, Florida, US.

S Omartian, The Power of a Praying Wife, 2014, Harvest House Publishers, Oregon, US.

T R Jennings, The God-shaped Brain: How changing your view of God transforms your life, 2017 IVP Books, Grand Rapids, MI, US.

T R Jennings, The God-shaped Heart: How correctly understanding God's Love transforms us, 2017 IVP Books, Grand Rapids, MI, US.

S Kendrick, Defined: Who God says you are, 2019, B&H Publishing Group, Nashville, Tennessee, US.

H Hurnard, Hinds' feet on high places, 1986, Tyndale House, Carol Stream, Illinois, US.

M Wells, Sidetracked in the wilderness: Find the way back to a victorious, abundant life, 2015, Abiding Life Press, San Diego, US.

About the author

Felicity Jayne is a published author and an exceptional storyteller with over 43 years of experience walking with Jesus. She has studied the Bible extensively, travelled the world, sitting on the banks of the Sea of Galilee, dipping her toes in the Jordan River, and walking through the gates of Jerusalem.

Refreshingly authentic, she brings the Bible alive, often referring to the Word as God's love letter from home. She is warm and funny, and her heart-warming encouragement and practical advice will help to inspire you to lean into a kind and loving relationship with the Heavenly Father.

Felicity Jayne has a special heart for women's ministry. She loves supporting women of all ages in her community.

Running ladies' groups and leading bible studies for over a decade, she knows how to uniquely engage and present to new and mature Christians alike, reminding us of God's incredible love and grace.

Through discipleship, she gives a unique look at some of the most challenging parts of being a woman. With experience as a wife, daughter, mother, and grandmother, serving in new people's and care ministries, she knows the busyness of life, the stresses we can face and the challenges of trying to do it all.

Let her show you God's love in a fresh, new way and remind you of the freedom that comes with following Christ.

For further copies of Free Indeed
or to access an eBook version place an order at

felicityjayne.com

Felicity Jayne is committed to speaking God's truth through love.

If you are keen to see how you can partner with her to speak to the gorgeous girls in your community,

contact her at

felicityjayne.com

FREE INDEED

www.ingramcontent.com/pod-product-compliance
Lightning Source LLC
Chambersburg PA
CBHW072154070526
44585CB00015B/1132